The St
English F

Bernard Price

Bernard Price began the study of antiques and fine art soon after leaving school, following a career as auctioneer and valuer until 1961 when he turned to writing and broadcasting. He rapidly achieved a national reputation through the BBC radio programme *Talking about Antiques*. His main interests are in art, literature and the countryside, and he is a regular contributor to such television series as *In the Country* and *The Antiques Roadshow*. As a lecturer he has travelled extensively throughout Britain and North America, and is now working on his tenth book.

The Story of English Furniture

Bernard Price

Edited by
Paul Smith
Anne Owen
Robin Drake

ARIEL BOOKS
BRITISH BROADCASTING CORPORATION

Acknowledgement is due to:
GEORGE ALLEN & UNWIN LTD for extracts from
'The Designer's Trade' by Sir Gordon Russell

Illustrations by David Brown

First published 1978.
This edition first published 1982
Reprinted 1983

Published by the British Broadcasting Corporation,
35 Marylebone High Street, London WIM 4AA

Typeset by Phoenix Photosetting, Chatham
Printed in England by Mackays of Chatham, Kent

Set in 10/11pt Linotron Ehrhardt

ISBN 0 563 16563 4

Contents

Chapter 9   Victorian Mainstream

Chapter 10   The Movement Forward

Chapter 11   The Twentieth Century

Appendix

Glossary

Index

British Monarchs

Henry IV and Henry V	1399–1422
Henry VI	1422–1461
Edward IV, Edward V and Richard III	1461–1485
Henry VII	1485–1509
Henry VIII	1509–1547
Edward VI and Mary	1547–1558
Elizabeth I	1558–1603
James I	1603–1625
Charles I	1625–1649
The Commonwealth and Protectorate	1649–1660
Charles II	1660–1685
James II	1685–1688
William and Mary	1689–1702
Anne	1702–1714
George I	1714–1727
George II	1727–1760
George III	1760–1820
Regency	1811–1820
George IV	1820–1830
William IV	1830–1837
Victoria	1837–1901
Edward VII	1901–1910
George V	1910–1936
Edward VIII	1936–1936
George VI	1936–1952
Elizabeth II	1952–

Foreword

I have been associated with the author, Bernard Price, on the Radio 4 programme 'Talking about Antiques' and have grown to rely on him for replies to questions on porcelain, pottery, books, pictures – in fact most questions except those on English furniture.

Now he has written a book on *this* subject and having read it I believe it will be the forerunner of many more about antiques. He feels 'at home' in telling readers the story of English furniture – not from the point of view of an expert but as an historian, recalling events that have happened in the past both domestically and nationally that have had great bearing on changing styles of English furniture.

I believe readers will learn to recognise the different periods and makers, learn to understand why certain kinds of furniture were made at given periods and learn to appreciate craftsmanship and design.

Bernard Price covers all periods in this book – designs from the Middle Ages right up to the present time – so everyone should find an interest within its pages.

Arthur G. Negus

Introduction

When I was a boy of sixteen I became a pupil in a firm of country auctioneers; it was the partners of this firm who first revealed to me the world of English furniture and who taught me to understand something of its craftsmanship, its changing styles and its social history. I remember very well the thrill that came from identifying timbers from their colour and grain; and the pleasure of recognising features of design. It was at that time that I learnt that the ability to describe an object is half-way towards an understanding of it.

In England today there is a growing interest in antique furniture. The fact that Britain has not been invaded or plundered for a thousand years – except by foreign collectors and dealers – has produced a tradition of handing on furniture from one generation to another; there must be tens of thousands of families in this country who own and treasure some of the furniture of the past. Yet every month some of it leaves our shores to satisfy markets in North America or Australia or Europe; one can only hope that with an increasing understanding of what is left, more English people – especially young people – will determine to keep what they have got and even to acquire more. Even though most of the furniture made before 1840 is beyond the reach of most people, I believe there is a growing appreciation of good Victorian furniture – and of that from later periods – so perhaps some of this, at least, may be saved.

No one book can do justice to the history of English furniture; it involves the history of England itself – of kings and queens, ordinary middle-class families, artisans and peasants; it includes journeys of exploration, the discovery of rare timbers, the complexities of trade and commerce, the great movements of European taste and the growth of craftsmanship. I can only hope that I have conveyed something of this complex saga.

Bernard Price

A 19th-century engraving showing sawyers using a sawpit, a method of sawing large timbers that continued virtually unchanged from medieval times until well into the 20th century.

1
Before 1600

Origins

The history of furniture is the history of the craftsmen who made it, their tools and skills and the timbers they used; and of the changing movements of style and taste that dictated its design and decoration. But it is also a record of the people who used it and their times. The splendid furniture of a great house creates a cumulative picture of all the generations who have lived there; and for the social historian, the simpler furniture of farms and cottages may be of still greater interest: the story it has to tell of domestic life in these anonymous households may well be the only record that exists.

In England in early medieval days such furniture was made by local craftsmen using native timbers – oak, beech, ash and elm; of these oak was the most popular and the one now most commonly associated with the period – just as walnut is associated with the reign of Queen Anne; but it is worth while bearing in mind that, though such associations can be useful as a rough guide in the dating of furniture, it is a mistake to apply them too rigidly. Walnut, for example, was also fashionable in the reign of Elizabeth I. But for the medieval joiner the choice of timber was not dictated by fashion; for him it was rather a question of the kind of tree that grew near his own back door.

Early furniture developed from the needs of domestic life itself; its form and variety were ruled by the tools and techniques available. The cabinet maker did not exist in medieval England; it was the age of the carpenter, the joiner and the turner, and they in turn depended on the sawyer. In a community of any size there was usually a saw-pit; timber was used for building houses and for a dozen other purposes as well as for making furniture and the sawyers must have worked almost round the clock.

In a peasant dwelling the furniture would certainly have been crude and probably cut directly from the log; but in all the furniture of that period lines were simple and surfaces frequently bore the marks of the tools used in their shaping. The effect of such honest labour was often to give life and vigour to the work of these early craftsmen and sometimes to lift it into the realm of art.

Not many examples of the furniture of this period are still in existence and what has survived is not always easy to date. Some designs were used again and again for generations – even for centuries; once they were proved to be practical they became virtually timeless. The three-legged stool, for instance, consisting of a circular top into which three splayed legs are dowelled right through and pinned from the top, was originally designed to cope with uneven earth floors. It is still being made today.

Safe-keeping

In almost every household the most important object was probably the chest or coffer; it served to keep clothes and blankets dry in houses where damp must have been a constant problem and it could double as a seat or a table – or even, at a pinch, as a bed. In the larger houses there might be several chests and in the most lavish it was the custom to put two in the bedrooms: a large one at the foot of the bed and a smaller one at the bedside.

Some of the most important examples of the medieval chest which have lasted until our own time were made to house the treasures of the church – to protect the altar plate from robbers and the parish archives from mice. Many English parish churches and cathedrals contain fine specimens. Among the earliest are the chests of the dug-out type, made by hollowing out a tree trunk and replacing the top section so as to form a domed lid. Early chests were often decorated with ironwork in the form of straps and hinges. Some of them date from Saxon times and they survived because they are practically indestructible – except perhaps by fire. Many of them are still being used today.

The chest in Chichester Cathedral is an outstanding example of thirteenth-century workmanship, with its heavy plank construction and decoration of chip-carved roundels; it is also fitted with a hinge unique to that period, known as a pin-hinge. In the deepest recesses of the carving it is still possible to see traces of the red ochre colouring that was originally applied. There is another fine example at Stoke d'Abernon church in Surrey.

In the reign of King John, Pope Innocent III issued an edict that chests should be placed in all the churches of England, for the contributions of the faithful to the funds of the fifth crusade. Some of these chests were fitted with three locks, each opened

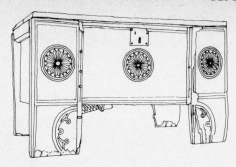

A heavy oak chest of plank construction, 13th century, decorated with chip-carved roundels. When new it was coloured with red ochre. Chichester Cathedral.

by its own key; the keys were entrusted to different key-holders, so that all three had to be present before the chest could be opened. Perhaps it was easier to part with one's money – even for such an ill-omened enterprise as the fifth crusade – when it was collected in so awe-inspiring a strong box.

Tables and chairs

Tables were originally no more than plain boards raised on A-shaped trestles at each corner, which could be dismantled when a meal was finished. Seating consisted of long benches and in the 'hall' type of house of the Middle Ages, in which the fire was in the centre of the room, the bench for the master of the house and his family and principal guests would have been placed against the wall so that their backs were supported and they could see the fire. By the end of the fifteenth-century building had improved and the hearth was more often sited in a chimney piece

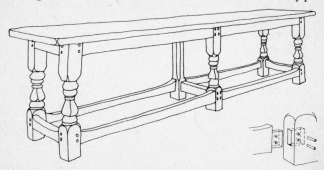

Refectory table, and detail of dowel fastening.

in the wall than in the centre of the floor. Accordingly, the trestle table and benches were moved out to dominate the centre of the room.

The next step was to produce a dining or refectory table of a more permanent kind, with the top fastened to legs and stretchers by dowels; some early oak pieces have the stretcher canted towards the sitter so as to provide a highly satisfactory foot rest. The floors in those days were strewn with rushes and straws, often dirty and even rat-infested, so any support that would keep the sitter's feet an inch or two clear would have been very welcome. The construction of the table was further improved by the Elizabethan invention of the draw leaf, which resulted in the first appearance of the extending dining table.

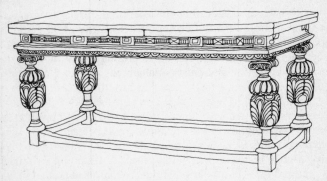

Elizabethan draw leaf table with richly carved cup and cover supports.

In the sixteenth century seats began to improve too. Although the bench continued to be used, long seats with backs came to be developed. These are known as settles; their evolution, however, probably owes less to the bench than to the chest which, of course, was also used as a seat. The settle, in fact, was virtually just a chest with the addition of arms and a panelled back. A similar influence can be seen in the development of some of the early chairs; with their simple frame and panel construction it is easy to see why they are often known as 'box chairs'. Other chairs of this period were made to an X-frame design that almost certainly originated in Italy. The stool remained popular but, by a natural adaptation, two of the supports were extended to form a chair of the type known as the 'back stool'.

The special importance of the chair is derived from the dignity and grandeur of the throne. All over the world the status of the

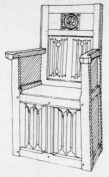

(Left) 16th-century joined oak 'box chair' with linenfold panels. The top panel is carved with a Romayne motif. (Right) Early chair of X-frame construction.

leader has always been emphasised by the place he sits and the chair he sits in. Even today the association has not been lost and at any meeting it is the chairman who presides. In primitive communities the seat of the chief is usually the seat in the shade – probably under a large tree; in the Far East the chair or litter of a high-ranking dignitary is shaded by a parasol. In North-western Europe the tree and the parasol were replaced by the canopy, which had the same symbolic meaning and which was often found above the thrones of kings and bishops. The tester on the four-poster bed has the same significance. The most notable of the early thrones still to be seen in England is the Coronation

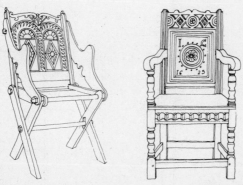

(Left) 'Glastonbury' chair – a design first used by the Abbots of Glastonbury and widely copied in the 19th century. (Right) Oak armchair, with reeded mouldings, 1625.

17

Chair in Westminster Abbey. It is carved in oak and, although it has no canopy, is decidedly architectural in form; it was made to the order of Edward I to hold the Stone of Scone, brought from Scotland in 1296.

Peace and security

England was at war almost without a break from 1339 until 1485 when the Wars of the Roses came to an end. They had lasted for thirty years; the respite from a century and a half of turmoil and above all from the bitter struggles of civil war brought with it a new security of life and outlook. Houses could now be built without the need for fortifications and the medieval hall gave way to long galleries and numbers of private apartments. Furniture began to assume a stability and permanence in keeping with the times. If this owed something to the improved techniques developed by carpenters and joiners, it probably owed even more to the new domestic habits of their patrons. For generations the court and the nobility had moved about the country, both on campaign and on their normal circuit of visits to their various estates, and furniture had been designed, in spite of its great weight, to be portable. Jointing with oak pins or dowels had made it possible to dismantle even the heaviest pieces. Now it was possible to set up house on a permanent basis; furniture, accordingly, was no longer constructed with travel in mind, and once it was installed in a room, it was expected that it would stay there.

Now that the demand for furniture was growing, so too was its variety. In the sixteenth century food cupboards became in-

Food cupboard with pierced and carved panels.

creasingly important; they were always made with pierced holes or cut decoration to provide ventilation. The smaller ones were usually known as hutches and the larger ones as livery cupboards – the word livery being used in those days to indicate the dispensing of food or an allowance of food to servants and retainers. The sideboard was at first precisely what its name implies, but by the end of the sixteenth century it had developed into the tiered buffet and the now well-known court cupboard.

Carved oak buffet or court cupboard with typical ornament.

Cupboards for clothes too, usually known as clothes 'presses', became increasingly popular at this period; and now that houses were being built with a number of separate bedrooms, there was a need for more beds. Even quite modest householders might own more than one four-poster; Shakespeare, for example, must have owned at least two as he left his second-best bed to his wife. It was Shakespeare too, who made the first known reference to what must be the most celebrated Tudor bed in England: the Great Bed of Ware. In *Twelfth Night*, which was first performed in 1601, Sir Toby Belch speaks of a sheet 'big enough for the bed of Ware'. This massive four-poster is now in the Victoria and Albert Museum: it was made, oddly enough, not for one of the great houses, but for an inn – most likely the White Hart at Ware in Hertfordshire.

In these more peaceful days there was time for the enjoyment of leisure and the arts; in some houses there was a special room where books were kept and read – a facility unknown until now

The celebrated 'Great Bed of Ware'. A superb example of Elizabethan carving with inlaid panels that are most likely the work of immigrant Flemish craftsmen.

outside schools and monasteries. Paintings came to rival tapestries in decorating the walls in private houses and a growing taste for display began to express itself in opulent clothes and in more luxurious and ornamental furniture.

Elaborate carving reached a peak in the reign of Elizabeth I; interlaced decoration was very popular and was often carved in the friezes of refectory tables. Decoration of this kind was known as strapwork and similar designs were used to great advantage in Elizabethan silver.

All mouldings and carved decoration were cut into the solid timber; unfortunately, many originally plain examples of Elizabethan furniture were to receive their carving at the hands of the Victorians. So all oak, even – or especially – that bearing an early date, should be viewed with some caution: close examination will often reveal the sharpness of Victorian carving. Where the piece itself is a blatant nineteenth-century copy, white edges can sometimes be seen where the staining has worn away. Where inlay was employed on early oak it usually took the form of the contrasting black and white of bog-oak and holly let into shapes cut out of the solid timber of which the object was made.

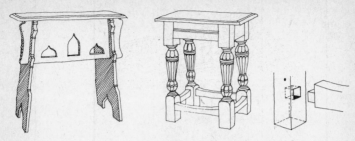

(Left) Stool of trestle form with Gothic piercing to underframe.
(Right) Carved joint stool, and detail of mortice and tenon.

Guilds and companies

The development of the foot-operated pole-lathe had marked the departure from earlier crude carpentry and a body of craftsmen had grown up in England who took great pride in their individual and collective skills. They were the turners. As early as the fourteenth century turners are mentioned in the City of London Records of the Trade and Craft Guilds; by the end of the fifteenth century they had acquired considerable power. Goods made by turners were rigorously examined at Turners Hall and there were tests to be passed, set by the Masters and Wardens, before a turner might describe himself as a master craftsman. In the early seventeenth century a Charter of Incorporation as a City Company was granted; that much we know – but the history of the Company before 1666 has been lost to us. Its records, like so many others, were destroyed in the Great Fire of London.

Yet another powerful group of workers employed in the construction of furniture were the joiners. The 'joyners of the City of London' were permitted to elect two wardens in 1440; they also had a number of provincial centres of which Chester and York were the most important.

The situation was further complicated by the organisation of carpenters, who developed in the fifteenth century from a Guild to a 'lesser Company' and to whom a Charter was first granted in 1477. Not surprisingly there were problems of demarcation between carpenters, joiners and turners. The bitter disputes over who did what job principally involved those working in London, since the provincial carpenter was expected to try and turn his hand to whatever was required of him. In particular, the carpenters working on large estates dealt with a wide range of work – a tradition that was to continue for centuries. It was of course the carpenter who was responsible for the construction of the timber frame houses of the medieval period, as well as for much of their furniture.

Later, in 1632, a dispute took place between the joiners and the carpenters which has been documented. It resulted in a decree by the Court of Aldermen that defined the items that should be manufactured only by joiners:

> All sorts of Bedsteads whatsoever (onlie except Boarded Bedsteads and nayled together).
> All sorts of Chayres and stooles which are made with mortesses or tennants.
> All tables of wainscotte wallnutt or other stuffe glewed with fframes mortesses or tennants.
> All sorts of formes framed made of boards with the sides pinned or glewed.
> All sorts of chests being framed duftalled pynned or glued.
> All sorts of Cabinets or Boxes duftalled pynned or glued.

The work of the turner developed rapidly through the sixteenth and seventeenth centuries with considerable improvements being made upon the wooden lathe of earlier times. The result was that turned or 'thrown' chairs, with the design possibly owing something to Scandinavian influence, were popular from the medieval period through to the reign of Charles II. During the seventeenth century the bulbous supports and shafts that had been so popular in Elizabethan times evolved into supports consisting of smaller turned knobs and balls; and the turned balusters and spindles into superb deeply twisted spirals.

 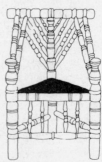

(Left) Foot-operated pole-lathe, a type used by many turners from Tudor times to the 20th century. (Right) Early turned chair of typical form.

The year following the quarrel between the carpenters and joiners produced another dispute – this time between joiners and turners. To resolve it the Court of Alderman defined that:

> turning and joyning are to several and distinct trades and we conceive it very inconvenient that either of these trades should encroach upon the other, and we find that the turners have constantly for the most part turned bedposts and the feet of joyned stools for the joyners and of late some joyners who never used to turn their own bedposts and stool feet hafe set on work in their own houses some poor decayed Turners, and of them have learned the feate and art of turning which they could not do before. And it appeareth unto us by custom that the turning of Bedposts, feet of Tables, Joyned stools do properly belong to the trade of a Turner and not to the art of a Joyner and whatsoever is done with the foot as have treddle or wheel for turning of any wood we are of opinion and do find that it properly belongs to the Turners.

The Continental influence

It was not only who-does-what disputes which bedevilled the English furniture industry; more than a hundred years earlier, Henry VIII's favour towards foreign traders had resulted in another familiar grievance: 'Dutchmen bring over iron, timber, leather and wainscot ready-wrought into nails, locks, baskets, cupboards, stools, tables, chests, girdles, saddles and painted cloths, so that if it were wrought here Englishmen might have some living and work by it.'

But Henry's interest in the world of Continental craftsmen was not merely commercial; he encouraged foreign trade and welcomed foreign merchants, but he also had a genuine interest in the arts and a great awareness of the artistic developments taking place across the Channel. This influence is of the first importance in understanding the evolution of sixteenth-century design and decoration. Early in the century the well-established Gothic and Tudor motifs and forms, such as the pointed arch and the linenfold panel, began to decline in popularity as the influence of Renaissance ideas from the Continent began to make itself felt. Perhaps the most easily recognised of the new motifs is the medallion head that began to appear in room-panelling and on furniture, particularly on cupboard doors and the backs of chairs. Entirely derived from Italian carving, it is known in England as 'Romayne' work.

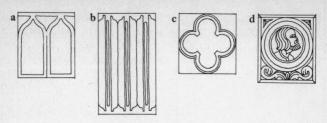

Early decorative motifs **a** *pointed arch* **b** *linenfold* **c** *quatrefoil* **d** *Romayne.*

Most of the Italian Renaissance designs reached England through Germany and the Low Countries and in the process underwent change: the printed pattern-books that arrived in Britain were even more florid than the original versions. In the reign of Elizabeth I, these designs were not exactly 'pirated', but they were seized upon and embellished yet again by the enthusiastic English woodcarvers. The bulbous turning that one sees in so many sixteenth-century supports was originally introduced from Flanders. At first it was retained as the plain Flemish bulb, but it clearly provided the perfect vehicle for the English carver to practise his art. The result was the development of the deeply carved cup and cover support that is perhaps most often associated with this period. Boldly carved caryatids such as those on the Great Bed of Ware also strongly demonstrate a Continental influence.

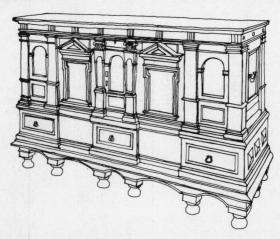

A chest, c. 1590, of the type often described as a 'Nonsuch' chest. The drawers in the base represent the first movement towards the chest of drawers.

The fashion for inlay advanced rapidly and this was no doubt partly due to the arrival in England of German craftsmen who favoured inlaid architectural views like those to be seen on the so-called Nonsuch chests – a fine example of which is to be found in Southwark Cathedral.

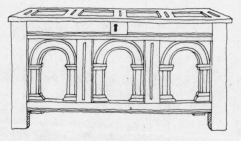

Carved oak chest with arcaded panels.

A free mixing of the traditional English style with bastard Renaissance resulted in many curious, and even audacious, juxtapositions of the two; yet a remarkable harmony was achieved more often than not. The flamboyance of Elizabethan chequered and floral 'cut-in' work, the bold carving and arcading, and above all the forthright robustness were entirely in keeping with the buccaneering spirit of the times.

2
Jacobean and Restoration

Furniture in the reign of James I

After the death of Elizabeth there were no immediate or dramatic changes in furniture development, but the accent was increasingly towards greater comfort and facility. In the more important farmhouses, manors and country houses, and in the towns, life was changing for the better. Heating, and in particular draught prevention, was far more satisfactory and fires were more safely contained. In some great houses it was boasted that the same fire had burnt in the hearth for over a century, such was the ready and free supply of timber from the English woods and forests.

Much of the timber was still sawn in the laborious saw-pits. But the process was slow; many furniture makers chose to cut smaller trees and to cleave them with wedges in order to save time and labour. The uneven cleft surface can still be seen on a number of pieces of pre-1700 furniture. While this practice suited many of the joiners, the felling of the smaller trees must have had a detrimental effect on the woodlands themselves.

From at least 1590 velvet and other coverings had been gaining in popularity for the upholstery of seat furniture of all kinds.

Farthingale chair.

'Turkey-work' was widely used: though of English manufacture this was, as the name suggests, copied from carpets imported from Turkey, and had been used as table coverings for many years. During the reign of James I upholstered furniture attained a level of luxury and comfort seldom to be achieved again before Victorian times. Probably the finest collection of very early upholstered furniture is to be found at Knole House in Kent.

Monk's bench.

New forms of furniture began to evolve. In one case the design was dictated by dress. A seat was needed which would accommodate the voluminous farthingale worn by the fashionable ladies of the period: hence the introduction of the 'farthingale chair', in direct line of descent from the back stool. The 'monk's bench' was another practical invention. It was in no way associated with monks; it consisted of a settle with a board at the back hinged to fold forward so as to form a table. A smaller version was constructed with a chair instead of a settle.

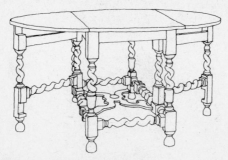

Carved oak gate leg table with X-shaped stretcher, c. 1670.

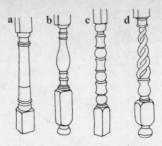

a *turned column* **b** *baluster turned* **c** *ball and reel* **d** *barley-sugar twist.*

By now the old custom of eating in the hall at a large heavy table, where precedence was strictly observed and guests and household sat either 'above or below the salt', was being abandoned in fashionable houses. People now dined at smaller tables in smaller rooms and for additional convenience a table was invented which could be folded. It came to be known as the 'gate leg' table, because of its hinged leg which opens like a gate to support a flap top. It was a great success and was soon being made by country craftsmen as well as by those in London. Those made during the reign of James I tend to have solid turned column legs, and the now more familiar table, having two gates instead of one, soon developed. From about 1640 we find turned baluster legs which, in the following twenty years, gave way to ball and reel turning. This was superseded not long after by the barley-sugar twist. While the more traditional form never really went out of fashion in the countryside, the eighteenth century saw the development of a much lighter table, still with two gates but now with very slender legs. Such tables are often referred to today as 'spider leg tables'.

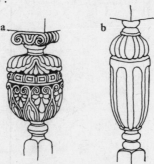

Comparison of cup and cover styles. **a** *Elizabethan* **b** *Jacobean.*

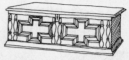

Bible box with sloping front on stand to form desk, and a more common rectangular Bible box.

One of the commoner articles to be found in the early seventeenth-century house was what has come to be called the 'Bible box'. Although many of these boxes would indeed have held a Bible, one can surmise that many were actually used for the safe-keeping of documents and other family treasures. They were by no means of uniform size but few are more than two feet six inches wide, two feet deep or ten inches high. A feature that has proved particularly attractive to the modern collector is the wide variety of decoration to be found on this one small item of furniture. Some boxes have a sloping lid, like a desk, but this is more likely to have been used as a book-rest than a writing surface. This design may have had an influence on the evolution of the locker desk but one has to bear in mind that at this date writing was still a comparatively rare skill.

Jacobean court cupboard showing plainer supports than those of earlier examples.

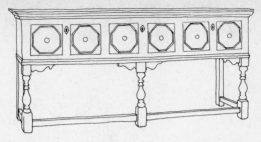

17th-century dresser.

The massive bulbous turning of the Elizabethan age was thinned down. The cup and cover supports became more elongated and carried less carving, and in many cases took on the appearance of a plain pillar support. The court cupboard continued to be made, but here again it was less elaborate, and often in later examples the turned supports in the upper half were reduced to mere inverted finials. Court cupboards went on being made, in fact, until the early eighteenth century in country areas. But in the farmhouse it was the dresser that was to develop into an article of major importance during the seventeenth century. Originally made without the separate tall back with shelves, it soon came to be made in the form known today by most people as the 'Welsh dresser', although there were many regional variations.

Charles I and the Commonwealth

During the reign of James I the evolution of design in England failed to keep pace with the rapidly changing tastes of the Continent. When Charles I came to the throne in 1625 he was clearly intent on moving English taste into the mainstream of Renaissance development. By inviting leading Continental painters to the English court as well as by his own aesthetic sympathies and his lavish expenditure on the decoration and furnishings of the royal palaces, he provided an all-round stimulus to artistic activity. But the Civil War put an end to the practice of the gentler arts and the Protectorate had no time for such frivolities. The chastening effect of Puritanism, however, did bring one compensation: now that decoration took second place to function in furniture, exaggerated luxury and ornament disappeared. Leather, for example, came into favour for upholstery during the Protectorate and many chairs that would otherwise have been upholstered in velvet or brocade were now panelled with leather instead.

Commonwealth period chair upholstered in leather.

Several practical innovations in furniture design date from this period. By the mid-seventeenth century we see the beginnings of the true chest of drawers, probably inspired by the earlier chest or coffer but now with one or two drawers set in the base. Early kinds are known today as 'dower chests' but at the time of their production they were called 'mule' chests – a term probably derived from their hybrid design.

From quite early on the drawers in some chests of drawers were graduated, which not only provided a choice in terms of storage but also helped the balance and general appearance. Even the clothes press, or wardrobe, became more useful and more interesting when drawers were added to its base. At about this time the simple chest began to decline in popularity.

Clothes press with panelled doors and drawers.

Now all mouldings were applied, as opposed to the Elizabethan practice of carving them in the solid; and one comes across a number of chests of drawers in particular, where the decoration consists of applied mouldings in simple geometrical designs.

Chest of drawers with fielded panels decorated with inlaid bone and mother-of-pearl, and applied split baluster ornament.

Although nobody really knows when the stick-back chair made its first appearance, it is a fair assumption that early versions were developing during the seventeenth century and there are certainly many examples still in existence which can be ascribed to the early eighteenth century. They are known today as Windsor chairs, although, like 'Welsh' dressers, they vary in construction and ornamentation from region to region.

The East India Company

An event that was to have far-reaching effects for the next three hundred and fifty years was the estabishment in 1600 of the English East India Company, which Queen Elizabeth had chartered on 31 December of that year. Until then trade with the Far East had been largely monopolised by the Dutch and the Portuguese. As a result of the ensuing clash of interests the English company prudently withdrew from Japan and concentrated its efforts upon India. Indeed the history of the British in India is essentially the story of the East India Company.

Nevertheless, lacquered objects from China and Japan were finding their way to Britain, as well as objects of Indian art, and

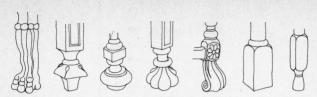

Typical foot shapes found in 17th-century furniture.

during the second half of the seventeenth century the Oriental taste in interior decoration was to dominate the fashionable interior. It also led to the production of 'japanned' furniture in Britain itself. Japan or japanning was a generic term given to all objects decorated with lacquer that had either come from or were in the style of the Orient; it did not signify that these pieces were from Japan alone.

It was natural that Europeans setting out to take up residence in India should take some of their furniture with them and in due course this inspired in India a tradition of Indo-European furniture, much of it produced in ebony. Ebony was among the most fashionable timbers of the seventeenth century; the black wood was a novelty and much sought after. It came mainly from Mauritius and India's Malabar coast, although another variety of ebony with a distinct reddish tinge was found in the Moluccas.

Commerce with India expanded fast and the East India Company sent an Ambassador, Sir Thomas Roe, who paved the way for lasting trade with the Great Mogul. Like other travellers before and since, he and his colleagues soon discovered the value of observing local customs:

> February 1615. The Embassy sent to the Great Mogul by the East India Company has been well received and very honourably entertained. Mr. Wm. Edwardes presented King James's letter and presents, a case of knives, pictures, bottles, looking glasses and a rich cloak. There is great hope of a profitable trade in those parts so long as a continued open hand be remembered to keep the Mogul and the gentlemen of his Court mindful of our merchants; thus we are to buy their laws with our monies.

The cane chair controversy

One of the most distinctive forms of furniture of the late seventeenth century was the cane chair and, not surprisingly, it was invented in India. In the Ashmolean Museum, Oxford, there is a carved ebony chair which originally had a cane seat. It was the gift of Charles II to Elias Ashmole. But although this Indo-Portuguese example with its lavish carving is rather splendid it bears little resemblance to the later and much plainer English cane chairs. During the Great Fire much fine furniture had been destroyed and there was an active market for this new, and at that time cheap, kind of chair with a caned seat and back. However, it was not long before a far more ornate chair began to be developed, and the cane chair makers found themselves producing cane chairs and other seat furniture for some of the finest houses in England. Although cane chair production was very largely based in London it would seem that other chair makers in the Home Counties began to react and follow the fashion.

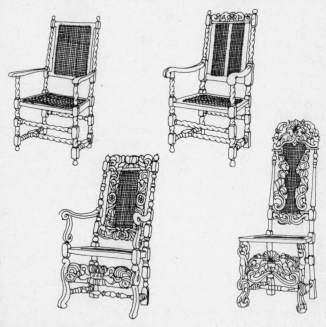

Four drawings that show the development of the 17th-century cane chair.

Carved decoration on these chairs involved flowers, foliage and bold scroll work. Frequently one also sees cherubim supporting a crown in the carving of the cresting rail. This is not just a symbol of enthusiasm for the Restoration; it also holds the deeper meaning that the crown and the monarchy were given by the grace of God.

Such chairs continued to be made well into the eighteenth century and the fashion was not lost upon a writer of the period; we find in Jonathan Swift's *Gulliver's Travels* published in 1727:

I desired the Queen's Woman to save for me the Combings of her Majesty's Hair, whereof in time I got a good Quantity; and consulting with my Friend the Cabinet-maker, who had received general Orders to do little Jobbs for me; I directed him to make to Chair-frames, no larger than those I had in my Box, and then to bore little Holes with a fine Awl round those Parts where I designed the Backs and Seats; through these Holes I wove the strongest Hairs I could pick out, just after the Manner of Cane-chairs in England.

As we have seen, early relationships between the various classes of artisans were not always of the best. The cane chair at the end of the seventeenth century dominated the market with the result that other chair makers and upholsterers found their work in decline and went so far as to petition Parliament to have a limit set upon cane chair manufacture. Cane chair makers were quick to reply and point out that:

about the Year 1664, Canechairs, &c. came into use in England, which gave so much Satisfaction to all the Nobility, Gentry, and Commonalty of this Kingdom, (for their Durableness, Lightness, and Cleaness from Dust, Worms and Moths, which inseparably attend Turkey-work, Serge, and other Stuff-Chairs and Couches, to the spoiling of them and all furniture near them) that they came to be much used in England, and sent to all parts of the World; which occasioned the Chair-Frame Makers and Turners to take many Apprentices; and Cane-Chairs, &c. coming in time to be Carved, many Carvers took Apprentices, and brought them up to Carving of Cane-Chairs, Stools, Couches and Squobs only: And there were many Apprentices bound only to learn Split the Canes, and Cane those Chairs, &c.

In 1690, Nicholas Barbon in his 'Discourse of Trade' summed up the situation with calm good sense, and in due course all talk of prohibition was dropped. He wrote:

The particular Trades that expect an Advantage by such Prohibition, are often mistaken; For if the Use of the most Commodities depending upon Fashion, which often alters; The Use of those Goods cease. As to Instance, Suppose a Law to

Prohibit Cane-Chairs; It would not necessarily follow, That those that make Turkey-Work Chairs, would have a better trade. For the Fashion may Introduce Wooden, Leather, or Silk Chairs (which are already in Use amongst the Gentry, The Cane-Chairs being grown too Cheap and Common) or else, they may lay aside the Use of all Chairs, Introducing the Custom of Lying upon the Carpets.

The Restoration

In the spring of 1660, Charles II came home. John Evelyn watched his entry into London:

the ways strewed with flowers, the bells ringing, the streets hung with tapisserie, fountains running with wine. . . . myriads of people flocking, even so far as from Rochester. I stood in the Strand and beheld it and blessed God.

It was like the end of an ice-age. The grey decorum of Cromwell's regime at Whitehall gave way to an opulence and frivolity unequalled at any English Court before or since; but the King's tastes had not been learnt in England. He was half French by birth and more than half by disposition and he had spent much of his youth in Paris. When he came home he and his entourage brought French fashions and French standards with them. The plays of Racine and Corneille were the models for English playwrights at the newly opened London theatres; the music of Lully was played at Court; the gallantry, the ostentation, the luxury of St Germain were faithfully copied there; and when in 1668 Louis XIV began to rebuild Versailles its splendours set a standard for English architects, painters and craftsmen. On both sides of the Channel it was a golden age for all the arts.

Ham House in Richmond was built in the early seventeenth century but much of the furniture dates from the reign of Charles II and reflects all the flamboyance of the period. From correspondence of the time it is clear that some of it was made by Dutch joiners who were also employed on the construction of the house. The parcel-gilt walnut tables, for example, with their female caryatid supports are rare in English furniture and are very likely the work of the foreign craftsmen. It is, however, difficult without firm documentary evidence to distinguish their work from that of English furniture makers.

There are several exceptional pieces of furniture in the house which form a commentary on the spirit of the times. Among the most important are two remarkable writing cabinets with silver

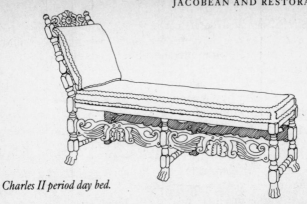

Charles II period day bed.

mounts, each on a stand with carved and turned legs. In the 1679 inventory of Ham House they appear as 'scriptors garnished with silver'. These fascinating pieces, with their fall-flaps in the manner of the escritoire, are something of a landmark in English cabinet work. Two 'sleeping chayres' of about 1675 are both dignified and comfortable as well as being extremely rare; a ratchet enables the angle of the back to be adjusted to suit the sitter, while the feet are exotically carved as sea horses. Other pieces well worthy of study in this house are the set of chairs with black and gilded frames upholstered in yellow satin and decorated with red cord appliqué. Very little fine upholstered furniture of this period survives in anything approaching reasonable condition, although there are other good examples again at Knole.

A 'scriptor' on carved and turned legs, c. 1679.

Libraries were apparently not uncommon in the larger houses of the early seventeenth century; book-shelves must therefore have been standard equipment. But the first reference to a domestic bookcase was made by Samuel Pepys in the year of the Great Fire. On 23 July 1666 he records: 'Comes Simpson the joyner and he and I with great pains contriving presses to put my books upon, they now growing numerous'. These presses were cupboards with hinged doors and grooves cut in the sides, so that shelves could be inserted at appropriate heights. Such was his passion for order that he put blocks under the books so that they all appeared to be of equal height. His books eventually grew so numerous that he had twelve presses made in all, the later ones having the shelves fixed because by this time Pepys had decided exactly how he wanted his books arranged.

One name which stands out in the history of seventeenth-century decoration is that of Grinling Gibbons. In one of the rooms at Petworth House in Sussex we can see his work displayed at its best. The pair of double picture frames flanking the chimney piece bloom with confidence and bold technique, with their cascades of flowers and fruit, classical vases and ducal coronets. Putti sound trumpets and musical instruments of all kinds take up the chorus. They are perhaps the greatest of the carver's masterpieces, and in the words of Horace Walpole 'the most superb monument of his skill'. Other fine limewood carvings in the same room are mainly by John Selden whose work owes much to that of the master.

Domesticated science

One of the characteristic creations of the seventeenth century was the Royal Society for the Improvement of Natural Knowledge, known to us simply as the Royal Society. It was founded in 1645 and Charles II, who was amused by scientific experiments, became its patron and granted it a Royal Charter. As its name implies, the Society fostered an all-embracing spirit of enquiry; its members were interested not only in establishing the natural laws of the universe but in finding practical solutions to everyday problems and many of their discoveries had an important bearing on domestic life and the domestic interior.

One of the most versatile of them was Sir Robert Hooke; he was interested in architecture and agriculture, he studied the habits of the cheese-maggot (observing that 'she puts her tail into her mouth and when she leaps, springs it out with great force, like a flea') and in 1665, he established the principle of the

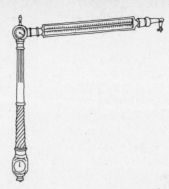

'Signpost' barometer.

'banjo' barometer, which was to be exploited in the following century. The first barometer had been invented in 1643 by Torricelli, a pupil of Galileo; five years after Hooke's discovery, Sir Samuel Morland produced a 'signpost' barometer; and in 1674, the excellent glass patented by George Ravenscroft furthered the development of all kinds of barometer and cabinet makers began to devise cases for them.

Furniture makers began to be interested in clock cases at about the same time, for the science of horology was developing rapidly too. Most of the early clocks in England were based on European originals, the hanging clocks and brass-cased lantern clocks of the sixteenth and early seventeenth centuries being wound by pulling lengths of chain on which weights were suspended. But in the late 1650's the first of several developments took place – the application of the pendulum as a regulator. Based on work started by Galileo, who had died in 1642, this was carried out by a Dutchman, Christian Huygens. The idea immediately caught on. The man who introduced it into England was probably Ahasuerus Fromanteel; an advertisement of 1658 refers to his manufacture and sale of pendulum clocks in this country. The old chains and cords were replaced by catgut wound on barrels, and the greater length of line enabled the clock to operate for eight days instead of the more usual thirty hours. Such clocks were driven by falling weights; others – mainly table clocks – took their power from a coiled spring. But both types were now fitted with short 'bob' pendulums.

The pendulum made a great improvement to time-keeping, but in a few years it was discovered that a long pendulum proved far more satisfactory than a short one. However, the great width of the arc of swing – unavoidable with the verge escapement then in use – was a stumbling block not to be overcome until the invention of the 'anchor' escapement in London about 1670. This brought both the arc of swing of the pendulum and the power needed to keep it going within acceptable limits.

The tall case that had in the meantime been devised to protect the weights and cords could now accommodate the longer pendulum as well; and so the long-case clock came into being. The modern term 'grandfather clock' only came to be used because of a popular nineteenth-century music-hall song. It gave the English cabinet maker another piece of furniture on which he could show his growing skills. The early long-cases have true elegance. Some were definitely architectural in design, while others had their front and sides worked with finely moulded panels and raised centres, carved and gilded capitals and twist-turned pillars. In the door of the trunk there was frequently a glazed opening or 'bull's-eye', framed with a moulding, so that the proud owner could enjoy looking at the movement of the pendulum – or check that it was still going. Soon many of them were decorated with lacquer work or veneered in walnut with floral marquetry and parquetry – all arts of the cabinet maker which were to flourish during the William and Mary period.

3
William and Mary

New incentives

In the December of 1664 a new comet appeared – a portent, it was said, of disaster. Within four months the Great Plague began and in the next year 13,200 houses were destroyed in the Great Fire of London. There were those who believed that this was a judgement on the licentious behaviour of the Court – though in fact Whitehall was spared; and the catastrophe was to bring its compensations. It cleared acres of slums and it gave an incentive to architects, builders and furniture makers as powerful as the Restoration itself.

In 1685 another calamity occurred which was to have important implications for English craftsmen. Louis XIV revoked the Edict of Nantes which had guaranteed religious toleration to French Protestants. By this piece of criminal folly Louis lost many of his most talented and industrious subjects. Over 400,000 Huguenots fled from the persecutions that followed – to Holland, Switzerland, America and England. They brought with them skills new to the English which improved silk weaving and upholstery, stimulated silver design and revolutionised joinery. New techniques of decoration were now emerging that were outside the range of the ordinary joiner, turner and carpenter; and we see for the first time the emergence in England of the cabinet maker.

Veneer and marquetry

Many German and Dutch cabinet makers were also encouraged to come to England by the accession, in 1689, of a Dutch king – William III. Most of these settled in London though some went to Norfolk; and the art they brought with them was that of using veneer and marquetry – although ventures in both these fields had already been made here during the reign of Charles II.

Many of the finest examples of William and Mary cabinet work are ornamented by roundels or 'oysters' of walnut or labur-

*Well-proportioned William and Mary walnut chest on stand with
characteristic inverted cup turned supports, shaped stretchers and bun feet.*

Double 'C' scroll support.

Upholstered chair and stool, William and Mary period.

William and Mary dressing or toilet table.

num. These were cut from the smaller branches of the tree. Transverse saw cuts were made straight through to provide roundels, while slices cut at an angle produced ovals, both methods showing the 'fan' of the grain to the best advantage. Indeed, the original term for veneer was 'faneer' for that very reason.

'Stringing' – a fine inlaid line of holly or boxwood – was often used to separate an area of oyster-shell pattern from, say, a reserve of marquetry. Another decorative feature was 'crossbanding'. This is a veneered border in which the grain runs cross-wise to that of the ground veneer. This is sometimes further enhanced by a banding of 'herring bone' pattern just inside it. Another attractive feature to be found mainly on pieces later in the period was the use of the 'burr' variety of walnut, with its tightly curled grain, which was obtained by cutting from the root area of the tree; an alternative source was the part where the branches join the trunk.

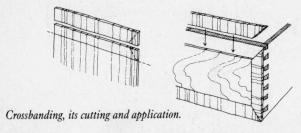

Crossbanding, its cutting and application.

Ebony, first introduced into Europe by the Dutch, had been rapidly exploited in their own furniture and in the furniture of France. Ebony, tortoiseshell, marble and brass were all widely used on the Continent in the creation not merely of matching

Walnut secretaire.

veneers, but of the pictorial cut veneers that we call marquetry. This work with ebony in France, particularly that of André-Charles Boulle, resulted in the French term 'ébéniste', a word which came to be applied to any cabinet maker whether he was working in ebony or not.

Although ebony was highly prized in England too, walnut was certainly the popular wood of the day.

It turned well, was tightly grained – taking on a high finish – and much of its attraction lay in its superb figuring. Even so, the use of marquetry began to predominate. Marquetry falls into two main categories: the floral, which was the first to be introduced here, and the arabesque, commonly and very appropriately described as seaweed marquetry. All manner of ornament was included in the striking and beautiful floral designs; the well-used acanthus-leaf scrolls which found favour in so many centuries, vases of flowers, vines and sometimes even birds.

Chest of drawers on stand.

It will be appreciated that the new marquetry was quite different from the inlay of the Elizabethan furniture using bog-oak and holly; that work is usually termed 'cut-in'. In marquetry a veneer cut from one type of wood is inlaid into the veneer of another in order to provide contrast of colour. The technique has deep roots, having been used in a rather different form by the ancient Egyptians, and, on a lesser scale, by the Greeks and the Romans. Eventually it emerged in Northern Europe, when ebony became the principal veneer.

One of the Dutch immigrants who had arrived before the accession of William of Orange was Gerreit Jensen – frequently anglicised later to Garret Johnson – who eventually became cabinet maker to the royal household. He adapted the arabesques from Islamic designs and also worked in the style of Boulle using brass, turtleshell and pewter. The word 'Buhl', incidentally, is usually used to describe later copying of Boulle's style of decoration, and it is worthwhile noting that most examples seen will belong to the early nineteenth century when a revival took place. Pure English marquetry was to achieve its peak in the second half of the eighteenth century when so many fine cabinet makers were under the influence of Robert Adam, and furniture of all kinds in mahogany and satinwood became the medium for Neo-Classical marquetry.

Repetitive patterns were also used in decorating furniture where a surface could be created by cutting and arranging geometric shapes to form a most pleasing overall effect. The term for such work is 'parquetry', and continues today in its baser form of the parquet wood-block floor. At its finest parquetry may establish illusions in perspective and frequently succeeds in achieving a three-dimensional effect on what is in fact a very flat, firmly glued surface.

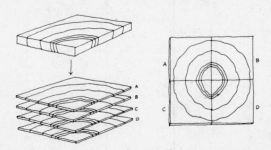

The cutting of quartered veneer.

Veneers in the seventeenth and eighteenth centuries were sawn by hand. Several methods for cutting them were used, but they all resulted in considerably thicker veneers than those cut by machine today. Even so, a fine craftsman would expect to saw eight slices of veneer from an inch of timber. When veneer was used in quartered designs, four slices were normally cut together.

The technique of marquetry

Marquetry could be produced in several ways, but the commonest was known as the 'sandwich' method. Slices of veneer of contrasting colours, along with one or two sheets of greased paper, were pinned together; this sandwich was completed by the addition of two rough off-cuts, one of them having pasted upon it, as a guide, a paper bearing the design to be reproduced. A fine saw was then used to cut out the pattern – the off-cuts preventing the saw from splitting or fraying the veneers and the greased paper lubricating the blade. The pieces cut out in this way were of identical shape but as they were in different coloured woods, one basic design would produce several versions of, say, a panel of flowers.

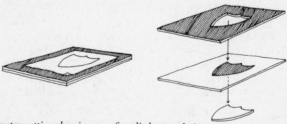

Marquetry cutting showing use of applied paper design.

Veneers used in this process were chosen with great care. Many varieties of wood were selected, and some were even given shaded effects by slipping the veneer into hot sand to scorch it. Veneers could also be dyed in order to provide extra colouring. Engraving on marquetry did not become fashionable until the second half of the eighteenth century.

When the selected pieces had been fitted to one another, the shaped area of the 'ground' – the surface of the carcase to be covered – was scraped and roughened and then coated with the best glue. The panel of marquetry was then laid and held with veneer pins, and a hot timber was clamped over the marquetry, which melted the glue beneath. The glue set again as it became cold and after 36 to 48 hours the clamp could be removed, although a week was usually allowed before it was finished and polished.

William and Mary marquetry 'Cushion frame' mirror.

Initially it was the craftsmen who could make the new marquetry-decorated cabinets who assumed the title cabinet maker, although John Evelyn had used the term as early as 1664. The training of apprentices moved on apace, and it was during the reign of Queen Anne that walnut furniture established itself at its best. Unlike other workers in wood – the joiners, turners and carpenters – the cabinet makers did not have a place among the city companies; neither did they have a separate guild of their own. However, the development of their skills and the growing pride in English cabinet work was noted by Evelyn. He said that 'from very vulgar and pitiful artists' they came to 'produce works as curious for their fitting and admirable for their dexterity in contriving as any we meet with abroad'.

Mirrors

A major factor in the furnishing and decoration of the grander houses was the increasing availability of mirrors. Mirror glass began to be manufactured in London at Vauxhall in the early 1660's, although it remained a very expensive commodity for many years; and George Villiers, second Duke of Buckingham, obtained sole rights to manufacture silvered glass mirror plates. With the growing production of mirror glass there came to be a demand for decorated frames. Silver, tortoiseshell, ivory and needlework were fitted to bare wooden mirror frames. Carved and pierced frames, in common with several other kinds of furniture, were decorated further by the gilder, who also worked on gesso – an amalgam of chalk and size. This type of work increased both in output and in quality. Layers of size, the first sealing the grain of the wood, were each allowed to dry before the application of the next. When these had built up to a sufficient depth the carver could achieve detailed work of the finest nature. After coats of burnishing size had been applied the piece was finally ready for the gilder.

The popularity of mirrors was not a sign of excessive vanity in the fashionable world; it had a practical basis. Mirrors, strategically placed, multiplied the power of candles which were the main source of illumination and so made it possible to read or sew in comfort after dark. Pier glasses flanked by tall candle-stands, known as torchères, transformed evening parties – particularly the card parties which were now so much in vogue. Gaming had been suppressed under the Puritans and revived, with enthusiasm, at the Restoration; it was to continue a ruling passion among the upper classes for well over a century. In the reign of William and Mary the first tables designed especially for card games were made.

Daniel Marot

One of the most important of the Huguenot designers who influenced English furniture in the late seventeenth and early eighteenth centuries was Daniel Marot. He was born in Paris in 1663, the son of an engraver. He embarked on a career as an architect, decorator and furniture designer; a career that was disrupted when, like so many other Protestants, he was forced to seek refuge in Holland in 1684. He entered the service of William, Prince of Orange, and served the Dutch Court.

Daniel Marot chair.

The Melville bed by Daniel Marot.

At the accession of the Prince to the English throne as William III, Marot described himself as architect to the King of Great Britain and the royal coat of arms appeared on a number of his pieces. He visited England from 1694 to 1698 and there is a record of payments to him during this stay of 1,800 guilders, taken to be evidence that he had worked on the gardens of Hampton Court Palace; he may well have been consulted on the decoration of the interior where numerous features are very much in his style.

His work was highly decorative and richly Baroque in character, and the English cabinet makers were quick to assimilate and make use of his designs. He was responsible for introducing far more life into the contemporary chair – favouring rich carving, tall backs and curved legs and stretchers. His furniture was in the French style of his day, and his designs for state beds are splendid creations of the Baroque. The first collected edition of Marot's designs made its appearance in 1702 and one design for a state bedstead is similar to the Melville bed, now in the Victoria and Albert Museum. Lord Melville was a minister of William III and his bed, with its headboard carrying his cypher and its hangings and cornice, is typical of Marot's taste. Very little detailed information exists concerning the work of Marot in England, and we know far more of the work of the many other Huguenot

49

cabinet makers who then were his colleagues and followers.

Eastern influences

In the second half of the seventeenth century there was a consuming interest in the products of the East. The fashion for collecting Oriental ceramics was led by Queen Mary herself and gave rise to the designing of cabinets fitted with glass doors to display the highly prized 'china'. The importation of Oriental lacquered furniture was quite unequal to the demand. The brightness and lasting qualities of the Oriental lacquer encouraged manufacturers in England to attempt substitutes. Their efforts were successful only to a degree and English lacquer never quite achieved the quality and brilliance of the Eastern originals.

The essential difference between the English and Oriental lacquers was that in the Orient gum was used from the lac tree, while the various coloured lacquers produced in England were based on varnishes. The much travelled navigator and hydrographer Captain William Dampier was fascinated by the gathering of lac, which he noted was:

> a Sort of gummy Juice, which drains out of the Bodies of Limbs of Trees . . . gotten in such Quantities by the Country People, that they daily bring it in great Tubs to the Markets.

In 1670 it was recorded that 'some artisans were sent out to introduce patterns suitable for sale at home'. Thirty years later the English joiners were protesting that:

> several merchants and others have procured to be made in London of late years and sent over to the East Indies patterns and models of all forms of cabinet goods and have yearly returned from thence . . . quantities of cabinet wares, manufactured after the English fashion.

The volume of imports was so large that the Joiners Company petitioned against it, stating that their own trade was 'in great danger of being utterly ruined'. But the threat to English cabinet work appears to have existed only in the field of lacquering itself, as Captain Dampier observed:

> the Joyners in this Country may not compare their Work with that which the Europeans make; and in laying on the Lack upon good or fine joyned work, they frequently spoil the joynts, edges, or corners of Drawers of Cabinets.

The lacquered case furniture that was imported from the East included desks, bookcases and kneehole writing and dressing tables; inscriptions in Chinese characters can often be found at the back of a drawer. All of these objects were now in growing use in this country. Seat furniture can also be included in the list of imports, and folding screens with incised lacquer designs found much favour in the seventeenth-century room. In 1682 Evelyn mentions a hall in the home of a neighbour where existed 'contrivances of Japan screens instead of wainscot'. This incised lacquer was known as 'Bantam' work. The Dutch East India Company had a trading station named Bantam in Java, and it was here that furniture decorated with this kind of lacquer work was collected for export.

English japanned cabinet on stand, with rich baroque carving. Late 17th century.

Japan in England

The term 'japan' or 'japanning' continued to be used to describe all this lacquer work whether it was of Oriental origin or not. In 1688 *A Treatise of Japanning* by John Stalker and George Parker made a great impact on the general public as well as on the professional cabinet maker. Stalker and Parker explain their japanning techniques very clearly and many amateurs have been enticed since its publication to follow their directions. In a reprint of the Stalker and Parker work in 1960, H. D. Molesworth states in his introduction:

> A page of Stalker and Parker and one is back in the Pepysian world of baroque London with its engaging self satisfaction, its provincial pomposity and its pretensions of classical learning.

Although it was a technical handbook it was enormously successful when it was published, and the following extract from the work is typical of its special charm:

> To lay Speckles on the drawing part of Japan-work, as Rocks, Garments, Flowers, &c.
>
> Before you can proceed to try this experiment, a little Sieve must be framed after this manner. Take a small box, such as Apothecaries employ for pills, something larger in compass than a Crown-piece, about half an inch deep; strike out the bottom, and in its place bind very straight about it fine Tiffanie, and to prevent coming off fasten it on the inside of your box with thread, and reserve it for your necessities.
>
> Now when your work expects to be adorned with Rocks, Flowers, or the like, use first your Pencil to varnish those places with, and whilst it is wet put some of your strewings into the Sieve, and gently shake it over the place designed for your Rock, until it appears answerable in Speckles to what you intended; but especially when for Rocks, call for a pencil about the bigness of your finger, one that is drie and new, and with it sweep all those stragling Speckles, that lie beyond the wet or varnished part, into the sides and top of the Rock that is thus moistened; for there it will not only stick, but render your work, thicker of Speckles in those places, more beautiful, and oblige it with a kind of shadow and reflection.
>
> This work admits of no idle hours, no interludes and vacations, for as soon as one part is compleated, the other desires to undergo the skill and contrivance of the Artist. When this Rock is drie, the next must succeed in operation; and by this way of working the one, when, and not before, the other is perfectly drie, you may, like the Giants of old fighting against Jupiter, cast mountain upon mountain, lay one rock upon or beside another, of different colours, and as many shapes, until the whole enterprise of Rock-work is completed. But observe, that in sweeping your Speckles into the edges of each Rock, you intermix not one portion of scattered parts into a Rock of a different colour; let them therefore enjoy their proper strew-

ings. When you thus lay your Rocks on your work being cold, it will certainly for the present look dull and heavy, nay to that degree, that you might very well suggest to yourself nothing less than the damage and ruins of the whole undertaking. But though no signs of life, beauty, or shadow do appear, let not this startle or discourage you; for when you have secured it, as we directed before, this fright vanishes, the dangerous Mormo or Bugbear disappears, its expected qualities suddenly arise, and by the assistance of your Securing varnish, it is decked with gay and beautiful apparel.

The quality of the lacquering on pieces of late seventeenth- and early eighteenth-century furniture is variable; it had become fashionable – perhaps as a result of Stalker and Parker's treatise – for the well-to-do to take up japanning as a pastime and it was not therefore produced exclusively by professionals whose livelihood depended on their skill. There is also sometimes considerable variation in the quality of the stands on which japanned and lacquered cabinets were set; some bear crude carving with pot-bellied putti in the Dutch manner, while others – presumably to suit more discriminating patrons – were made in the French tradition, with genteel balusters and swags of fruit and flowers.

By the end of the seventeenth century English cabinet makers were finding a market for their furniture in many parts of the world including Europe, the Turkish Empire and North America. Although their work was still remarkably unpretentious in comparison with the more ornate European work, the English cabinet makers were achieving a reputation for sound craftsmanship.

4

Queen Anne and Early Georgian

The coming of Classicism

With the dawn of the eighteenth century England began to enjoy a new prosperity. Trade was booming at home and abroad, farming flourished and fortunes were being made in speculative building. Owners of London property did particularly well, for London, with its half million inhabitants, was expanding rapidly – the commercial and industrial areas to the east and the fashionable dwelling houses to the west. Here the aristocracy lived during the Season but by midsummer most of them were back on their country estates; and here too they were soon building – pulling down their ancestral mansions and putting up new houses in the Palladian manner; or simply adding a Classical wing or so to the existing fabric.

A magnificent cabinet in walnut veneer with floral marquetry, c. 1700.

In 1715 Lord Burlington returned from the Grand Tour. Like most of his class at that time, he had been sent to the Continent to finish his education – to broaden his outlook and polish his manners and also of course, to study European art. Many of his contemporaries returned with packing cases full of treasures; Lord Burlington came back with a consuming ambition – to transform English architecture. He had fallen in love with the work of the Italian Renaissance designer Andrea Palladio. In the previous century Palladio's ideas had had a profound influence on Inigo Jones; now his *Four Books of Architecture* were published in English translation and these, combined with Burlington's enthusiasm, swung English building on to a new tack. The Baroque ideas of the previous age began to seem theatrical and extravagant and the patrician families caught up in the building boom came to prefer the clarity and balance of Palladio's designs.

Anything that smacked of excess – whether in architecture, decoration, manners or morals – was now considered vulgar. Elegance and 'good taste' were the ideals of the period and the new Palladian mansions made a perfect setting for their display. In furniture over-ornamentation, particularly in carving, was out of date; the elaborate loops and swags, the florid grandiloquence of the late seventeenth century, disappeared. The new furniture had a more formal delicacy in keeping with Classical 'correctness'.

Queen Anne chair carved and veneered in walnut, c. 1715.

Queen Anne furniture

The new era was heralded by the superb hoopback chair which is particularly associated with the reign of Queen Anne, though it continued to be made after her death. The chair's solid splat back, carefully shaped to fit the curve of the sitter's spine, the rounded front rail of the seat and the cabriole legs – newly introduced from the Continent – gave these pieces a remarkable and most satisfying symmetry. Such chairs did not need the hitherto

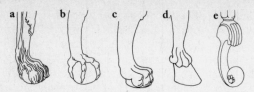

Feet employed during the first half of 18th century. **a** *hair foot* **b** *claw-and-ball* **c** *paw foot* **d** *hoof foot* **e** *scroll foot*

obligatory stretchers; and the cabriole leg might finish in a club, a claw-and-ball or even a foot of hoof form.

Chests of drawers, bureaux, bureau-bookcases and cabinets also began to shed earlier forms of support; ball and bun feet gave way to the bracket feet that were to evolve with a number of variations as the century progressed.

By the early years of the eighteenth century bookcases were to be found in most houses of any size. But the furniture of Queen Anne's reign is perhaps best exemplified by the magnificent composite pieces such as the bureau bookcase, the bureau cabinet and the cabinet on chest. These tall, often double-domed cabinets with their fine mouldings and beautifully chosen walnut veneers are a fitting inauguration of the Golden Age of English furniture. They are as splendidly finished inside as out; the timber, well-seasoned and well-dovetailed, producing draw-ers that fit as well today as the day they were made. They are

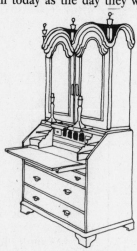

Double dome walnut bureau bookcase or writing cabinet, with candle slides, and on bracket feet. Early 18th century.

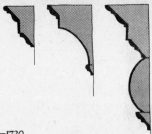

Cornice shapes, 1700–1730.

completed by well-designed escutcheon plates and elegant handles; what is more, as further proof of his skill, the cabinet maker sometimes added cleverly concealed secret drawers.

The evolution of the drawer

Although the design and decoration of any piece of furniture are of primary importance in assigning a date to it, the details of its construction can be helpful too. The techniques used in the making of drawers, for example, varied considerably over the years.

Early drawers usually had grooves cut into the sides which acted as runners. In the very late seventeenth century and the early years of the eighteenth, a moulding was frequently applied around the drawer-opening on the carcase of the piece itself; that is, on the partition edges. But then the drawer-front became about a quarter of an inch longer all round so that it projected and overhung the drawer-opening on all sides. From about 1730 onwards 'cock beads' were let into the front edges of drawers; this had the effect of providing a simple decorative feature while its main constructional purpose was to protect the veneer round the edges of the drawer-front – which now receded flush to the drawer-opening itself. The cock bead remained in high fashion until the end of the eighteenth century; its place as a decoration was largely taken by boxwood stringing, which continued to be used until the second quarter of the nineteenth century.

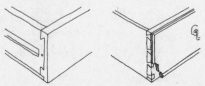

17th-century drawer with crude dovetails, thick side and running groove; and drawer c. 1730 showing greater sophistication and cockbead.

Early 18th-century walnut chest upon chest or tallboy. Points of particular note are the bracket feet, the sunburst, the fluted canted corners and the slide at the top of the lower section which could be pulled out and used for brushing clothes on.

Early 18th-century card table.

Bachelor chest with flap top.

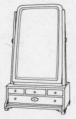

Toilet mirror in walnut veneer, early 18th century.

Queen Anne dressing table.

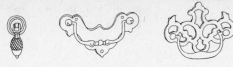

Brass drop-handles typical of the Queen Anne period.

In most pieces made before about 1730 the bottom board of the drawer shows the grain of the timber running from front to back; from about that date onwards the grain usually runs from side to side. In the space of the hundred years between about 1650 and 1750 dovetailing became progressively more delicate; this was not a sign of weakness, although certainly the drawer sides also became remarkably thin in the eighteenth century, but rather an indication of increasing refinement in craftsmanship. A common feature of nineteenth-century drawer construction is a rounded dust bead neatly filling the corners of the drawer between bottom and sides.

William Kent

As the century went on architects came to exert more and more influence over the contents of the houses they built; they made their own designs for furniture and taught cabinet makers to carry them out; and cabinet makers in their turn began to realise more than ever before that furniture should be designed to complement the decoration of the rooms in which it is to be set. The demand for fine furniture was country-wide and the new styles were dispersed from London to the provinces by the architects and their patrons so that a number of smaller towns became furniture making centres of some importance.

One of the most versatile of the early eighteenth-century architects and designers was William Kent. He was born in 1685

Giltwood settee by William Kent.

of very humble parentage but means were found for him to travel in Italy to study painting. During his stay there, which lasted from 1710 until 1719, he met several men of great influence, notably Thomas Coke, later Earl of Leicester, for whose collection Kent bought pictures and sculptures. In London he worked as a painter for Lord Burlington and published a book on the designs of Inigo Jones.

Kent then turned all his energies into architecture, interior design, furniture design and landscaping. He planned his gardens so that successive vistas unfolded one by one and he brought the same visual concept to his interiors where the eye was led gently from one decorative feature to the next. He enjoyed great houses and great rooms and his furniture is also in the grand manner; he clung, rather longer than most of his contemporaries, to the Baroque and his designs were therefore decidedly architectural. The domed top of Queen Anne's reign gives way to the broken pediment; his carved mouldings and his other enrichments are full of masks and foliage. Walpole described it all as 'immeasurable ponderous' and seen out of context, perhaps it is; but seen in the grand rooms for which they were designed, these pieces convey an impression of sumptuous splendour.

Walnut and mahogany

The first thirty years of the eighteenth century was a period of walnut veneers, gesso and marble tops; and amongst the walnut there are two varieties that stand out with great brilliance in English furniture. These are the red walnut from Europe and the Virginian or black walnut from North America. By comparison with these English walnut, except when cut in areas of close grain, is almost a shadow in terms of colour. Although the importation of walnut from France had begun in the early seventeenth century it was brought in on a much larger scale after the Restoration, and it was clearly a timber which the Court in exile had greatly come to admire. As Evelyn, in his *Sylva* in 1664, comments:

> were the timber in greater plenty amongst us we should have far better utensils of all sorts for our Homes, as chairs, stools, bedsteads, tables, Wainscot, cabinets etc. instead of the more vulgar beech.

According to tradesmen's accounts the walnut is often described as 'Grenoble wood' or 'French walnut-tree'. It was much liked by the English cabinet makers and it must have come as a severe blow to them when the devastating winter of 1709 destroyed most of the walnut trees in central Europe. The result, due to the scarcity in France itself, was the prohibition of its export in 1720. The gap created in England by the disappearance of such a fashionable timber was soon filled. The black walnut of Virginia began to be imported in regular quantities, and a great deal of exceedingly fine furniture was made from this.

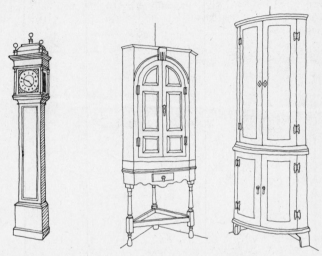

(Left) Long-case clock by Thomas Tompion, veneered in walnut, c. 1703.
(Right) Corner cupboards. Two very different but popular styles.

But it was yet another new timber that was to make the greatest impact on English furniture. It came from the Americas and it was called mahogany. It had been seen in England even in the seventeenth century when it was carried as ballast in ships; and in 1622 when Catherine of Braganza married Charles II, her dowry included not only Bombay and Tangiers, but also a large cargo of mahogany. From about 1720 onwards it began to be mentioned in advertisements and bills of lading and by 1724 a few pieces of mahogany furniture were actually being manufactured here.

In 1721 the duty on mahogany imported from the British Colonies in North America and the West Indies had been abolished – though this had been done to help the shipbuilders rather than the furniture makers. It was not until 1730 that large supplies began to arrive in England and that came chiefly from San Domingo. The wood was heavy, straight-grained, very hard and dark in colour. It was imported from Cuba too and much of the later mahogany from there had very fine figuring and included, for example, the renowned 'fiddleback'. Indeed this Cuban mahogany perhaps yielded the finest specimens of all and it tended to be reserved for veneers. With good well-tempered tools it could be worked easily and gave a splendid finish – at times even resembling bronze. In the second half of the eighteenth century, however, the lighter, more open-grained mahogany from Honduras in Central America came to be the principal timber used by cabinet makers. The ability to distinguish the Cuban or 'Spanish' mahogany from that of Honduras can be of considerable use in dating specimens of furniture.

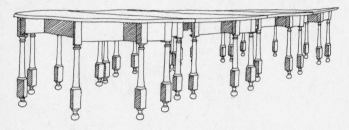

Early four-section mahogany dining table.

The major economic boost to the popularity of mahogany in England occurred in 1733 when Sir Robert Walpole abolished the import duty on timber altogether. (Not surprisingly perhaps, Sir Robert had mahogany used for the panelling of his own house at Houghton in Norfolk.) At first there was little change in styles: pieces of identical design were made in either walnut or mahogany. But it was soon realised that there was a significant difference in the properties of the two woods. The decorative value of walnut was its figuring which was seen at its best in the arts of veneering, crossbanding and quartering; and initially the mahogany that was imported was rather plain in its figuring and clearly more appropriate for use in the solid.

It was not long before furniture makers began to take advantage of the opportunities for changes in design that the new wood offered. The strength of the timber made it possible to use large expanses of mahogany board to make, for example, leaves for table tops; large boards could carry extensive pierced decoration

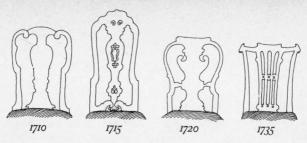

1710 *1715* *1720* *1735*

Development of chair back styles.

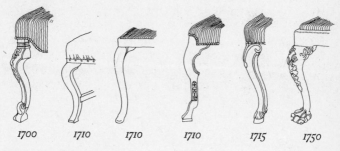

1700 *1710* *1710* *1710* *1715* *1750*

Development of the cabriole leg.

without jeopardising the strength of the structure; and carving came back into fashion, though it was a very different kind from that of the late seventeenth century.

The chair provides a good example of the developments that took place now that mahogany was in general use. In the early eighteenth century, with its shaped splat of solid walnut, it had tended to present a rounded outline. As the century progressed the top or cresting rail flattened and the line became broken; the uprights at each side of the back became less sweeping and the use of mahogany made it possible to construct a centre splat that could be elaborately pierced and carved. The leg, which in Queen Anne's time had either been plain or decorated with a simple shell ornament on the knee, now became more ornate as well. The knee carving, which was often very deep, frequently reached up to the ear-pieces where the leg joined the seat. In the reign of George II the cabriole leg was still popular; but new motifs made their appearance, the most common being the lion or human mask, the satyr, the cabochon and leaf ornament. The claw-and-ball foot was still in fashion but the paw foot and the scroll foot were alternatives sometimes used at this time.

A house in Holborn

By 1727 when George II came to the throne, the Middle Classes were on the move. The class system in England had always been flexible compared with those on the Continent and the merchants, still the driving force of the English economy, did not find it hard to buy their way into the ranks of the gentry. At the same time many other occupations were improving in status too; and doctors, actors, teachers and lawyers, who had once been despised as journeymen and parasites, were now accorded professional standing. The Bar in particular was the high road to wealth and nobility and barristers, as Soame Jenyns put it, often vied 'with the first in the Land in their houses, table, furniture and equipage'.

An auction sale catalogue dated 1730 gives a revealing impression of the furnishing of what was probably a typical middle-class house in London at that date. The house belonged to Henry Tomson Esq., of the Inner Temple, a barrister-at-law, and was described as his 'late dwelling house, Bartlet's Buildings, against the end of Hatton Garden, Holborn'. What appears to be the reserve price is printed after each lot, followed by a price handwritten in ink, which is probably the figure the lot reached at the auction.

The following are some items that came under the hammer:

In the 'best Chamber and Closet' we find:	Printed figures			Written figures		
A bedstead and sacking, with crimson silk damask furniture and counterpane	£20	0	0	£25	0	0
A fine Flanders tick feather bed, bolster and pillows	2	10	0	3	4	0
An India pattern callicoe quilt	0	15	0	1	3	0
Four India back walnut-tree chairs with stuff silk damask seats	2	2	0	2	13	0
A fiNE SILK PERSIA CARPET	5	5	0	—		
A walnut-tree writing-table with drawers ...	1	1	0	1	14	0
A chimney glass with a glass frame and a pair of glass sconces with glass arms	1	5	0	1	12	0
A stove and brass fender, shovel, tongs, poker and brush	0	15	0	1	4	0
A fine worked mahogany frame finished with sprig work	1	1	0	—		
Two worked square stools with loose cases	0	7	6	0	15	0
A strong box garnished with brass	2	2	0	—		

In the 'Fore Parlour' we find amongst other lots:

Two pairs of yellow callimanco window curtains, vallens and rods	£0	8	0	£0	17	6
A mahogany oval table	1	5	0	2	4	0
Six walnut-tree chairs with matted seats	0	10	0	3	1	10
A mahogany corner cupboard	0	8	0	1	5	0
A Japan corner cupboard		—			—	
A six-leaf India screen	1	0	0		—	
A pier-glass in a black and gold frame	1	15	0	3	0	0
A steel stove with fender, shovel and tongs	0	15	0	0	15	0

In the Dining Room there were:

Three pairs of chintz curtains lined with white callicoe, white vallens and pulleyrods	£1	11	0	£2	7	0
Seven walnut-tree chairs with leather seats and elbow ditto	3	0	0	6	10	0
A large sconce in a walnut-tree and gold frame with brass arms	2	10	0	3	18	0
A mahogany oval table	1	5	0	1	15	0
A battle piece in a black and gold frame		—			—	
A nobleman half-length by Rembrant		—		0	15	0
A chimney glass in a walnut-tree and gold frame with brass arms	1	11	6	2	0	0
A large Turkey carpet	1	10	0	3	5	0

In the wine vault there were to be found the following: 'part of a barrel of anchovis', six bottles of 'old hoc', five flasks of 'French claret' and two dozen cider, and a half-chest of 'Chiantry Florence bright and of a good flavour'.

It is a pity that the cataloguer makes no reference to the design of particular pieces, but one can clearly see from this very evocative list that the items represent several styles and periods. After all, this is what one might expect: pieces were not discarded or broken up because they no longer conformed to the latest fashions.

The use of the word 'India' is of some interest. It was used in the seventeenth and eighteenth centuries as a term to cover all Oriental goods, including of course lacquer furniture. The rather hazy state of geographical knowledge meant that the words 'Indian' and 'Chinese' were virtually synonymous in the minds of most people; and further confusion arose from the fact that nearly all imports from the Far East came via the East *India* Company.

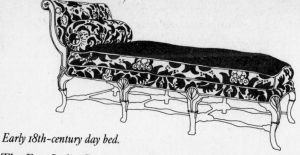

Early 18th-century day bed.

The East India Company had made progress in trade with China when in 1657 Cromwell granted a new charter. In 1715 when the company opened a 'factory' at Canton trade improved further and in the span of a generation England had become the most important trading nation in the world. Imports were brought into London and auction sales of cargoes were then held at East India House, the Company's headquarters in Leadenhall Street. Careful note was made in the accounts to distinguish between lacquered goods of East and West: 'right Japan' indicated Oriental lacquer, while 'japan' described the European production.

Furniture of the mid-eighteenth century

In 1753 William Hogarth in his *The Analysis of Beauty* proclaimed the gentle serpentine curve as the 'line of grace'. It was very much the line of the day as far as furniture was concerned. The rather heavy designs of William Kent, which look sometimes as though they were meant to be carried out in masonry or marble, were now counterbalanced by the exuberant freedom of the Rococo and once more the emphasis was on fluency and elegance rather than on solidity and strength. The massive cabriole legs and claw-and-ball feet on the bold furniture of George I and George II – the legs and feet of a mountaineer – were replaced by the graceful legs of a dancer.

By this time firms of cabinet makers had become highly organised; they pursued their skills as cabinet makers but now combined their activities with those of the joiner, upholsterer, gilder and chair maker. Most of the kinds of furniture that we are familiar with today had appeared, although there are one or two exceptions, and in a *General Description of All Trades* published in 1747 it was stated of cabinet makers that:

> many of their Shops are so richly set out they look more like Palaces, and their stocks are of exceeding great value.

The full potential was at last being developed. Wing armchairs, frequently covered in fine needlework, were rare in the late seventeenth century. Through the reign of Queen Anne and onwards they increased in popularity. Good upholstery, whether in tapestry or velvet, was always a feature, and finer examples of these chairs have cabriole legs with shell carving on the knees. Today such chairs are rare and they were obviously highly regarded; many accounts refer to them as 'easie chairs'.

Walnut winged chair, c. 1720.

The chairs of William Kent have been described by some authorities as having a 'throne-like' appearance, and such a description can as easily be applied to his settees which are especially suited to Palladian surroundings. Settees and sofas are divided by definition in that a sofa is sufficiently large for a person to recline in, whereas a settee is a seat to hold at least two people. The early seventeenth-century settees at Knole are the oldest to be seen in England, and by the end of that century settees were fairly common. Once again, they are enhanced with fine needlework coverings. In the early eighteenth century Soho tapestry, as well as being hung on walls, was used for covering the seats and backs of chairs.

Formal but well-upholstered two-seater settees are frequently termed 'love-seats'. From about 1720 onwards settees of double and triple chair form became fashionable, and these vary greatly in the amount of decoration they carry. Pieces dating from the 1740's are usually in mahogany while earlier examples are found superbly veneered in walnut with fine carving on legs and arms.

As usual it was the social and domestic habits of the rich that created a demand for new kinds of furniture. The eighteenth century was an age of immense dinners. Visiting foreigners were

Settee of double chair form veneered with figured burr walnut.
Early 18th century.

deeply impressed and sometimes a little appalled by the suicidal diet of the English. Even Parson Woodforde, who held a fairly modest living in Norfolk, thought nothing of entertaining his neighbours to 'fish and oyster sauce, a nice piece of boiled beef, a fine neck of pork roasted and apple sauce, some hashed turkey, mutton stakes, pork and mutton pies, salad etc., a wild duck roasted, fried rabbits, a plumb pudding and some tartlets, desert . . .' By Chippendale's time in the 1750's dining tables were well suited to these gigantic meals; they were large and often had folding leaves for extension.

Three-tier dumb waiter.

Dinner was taken at two or three o'clock at the beginning of the century and at five or six towards the end of it. When it was over the ladies would withdraw and a long bout of toasts would begin, the gentlemen occasionally relieving themselves in a chamber-pot kept in a sideboard drawer. The servants were sent away and the company were served from wine coolers and dumb waiters; the dumb waiter was an English invention which generally consisted of three circular or shaped trays round a central pillar. These trays were graduated in size from a large one at the bottom to a much smaller one at the top while the pillar support was mounted on a triple foot. It usually stood at the corner of the table where it was used for holding plates and cutlery as well as food and drink. Later in the century Sheraton produced several complex variations of this simple design.

Ladies often breakfasted in their bedrooms – usually on chocolate or tea and bread and butter – and a variety of breakfast tables were designed. Bedrooms also contained night tables or pot-cupboards and there was an increased demand for dressing tables as hair styles – and make-up – became more elaborate. Later, incidentally, many dressing table designs were adapted as the basis for writing desks.

In Georgian times ladies in England adopted the Continental habit of inviting their admirers to their 'levée' – the last stages of their toilette – and bedroom and dressing room furniture was therefore on show. Chests of drawers were still popular but tall-boys became fashionable as well. They were often veneered in mahogany of a good colour and the canted corners decorated with Chinese lattice work; they presented a more unified and elegant façade than the earlier chest upon chest.

In halls and drawing rooms console tables were now an established fashion – finished perhaps with colourful tops of 'pietra dura' or scagliola, if their owner had acquired a taste for that sort of thing on the Grand Tour.

Tea had become a national addiction. It was drunk at all hours of the day and Fanny Burney's mother once made Dr Johnson twenty-two cups in succession; but the formal 'tea-time' was after dinner and the ceremony had its own increasingly elaborate ritual, its own equipage and of course its own table. Indeed what Cobbett called 'the slavery of the tea and coffee and other slop-kettle' was responsible for new designs in silver, porcelain and furniture.

5
Thomas Chippendale

The 'Director'

Hanovarian England was by our standards rapacious, snobbish, gluttonous, often brutal and sometimes corrupt; it was also one of the most creative societies in our history. An age that produced Reynolds and Gainsborough, Gay and Garrick, Blake, Goldsmith and Jane Austen can stand comparison even with that of Queen Elizabeth. And creative talent did not end with the arts; scientists like Priestley and Jenner, inventors like Arkwright and Watt, designers and craftsmen like Wedgwood and Chippendale all lived and worked under the Georges.

Josiah Wedgwood and Thomas Chippendale had more in common than talent; they both realised that there was a great new market waiting to be exploited and both created designs that were perfectly timed to meet contemporary needs. Wedgwood, who was an entrepreneur on a grand scale, had at first aimed his high-powered sales organisation at the aristocracy; having scored a direct hit, he wrote: 'The Great People have had these Vases in their Palaces long enough for them to be seen and admired by

Chippendale carved mahogany armchair based on a design in the 'Director', 1762.

Chippendale period serpentine-front chest.

the Middling Class of people, which class we know are vastly, I had almost said infinitely, superior in number to the Great.' Much of what was offered for sale was either too crude or too grand for the 'Middling Class' and Wedgwood by his shrewd assessment of their needs, made himself half a million pounds.

Like Wedgwood, Thomas Chippendale seemed to set his name like a hall-mark on his own designs and his most valuable legacy is the book in which they are actually recorded. Various collections of designs and engravings had been published during the previous two hundred years but nothing on the scale of *The Gentleman and Cabinet Maker's Director* had ever been attempted before; and the engraved illustrations convey all the quality and strength of construction so beautifully masked by the elegance of the design and the carving. But Chippendale was a human designer in the best sense of the word: in addition to strength and elegance he also provided comfort.

Although the *Director* is the principal source of reference for Chippendale's work, the examples of his furniture which survive together with the accounts which refer to them are historically extremely important. The accounts for Nostell Priory (1766–1770) and for Harewood House (1772 onwards) describe the furniture in considerable detail; and we can still see the pieces in the positions for which they were originally ordered.

Chippendale's book was printed for him in London in 1754; and as well as being handled by a number of book sellers, it was also sold from his house in St Martin's Lane. Its impact upon his contemporaries can perhaps be guessed by reading his own preamble:

Being a Large Collection of the most Elegant and Useful Designs of Household Furniture in the Gothic Chinese and Modern Taste: including a great Variety of Book-Cases for

Libraries or Private Rooms. Commodes, Library and Writing-Tables, Buroes, Breakfast-Tables, Dressing and China-Tables, China-Cases, Hanging Shelves, Tea-Chests, Trays, Fire-Screens, Chairs, Settees, Sopha's, Beds, Presses and Cloaths-Chests, Pier-Glass Sconces, Slab-Frames, Brackets, Candle-Stands, Clock-Cases, Frets, and other Ornaments. To which is prefixed, a Short Explanation of the Five Orders of Architecture, and Rules of Perspective; with Proper Directions for executing the most difficult Pieces, the Mouldings being exhibited at large, and the Dimensions of each Design Specified; The Whole comprehended in One Hundred and Sixty Copper-Plates, neatly engraved, Calculated to improve and refine the present Taste, and suited to the Fancy and Circumstances of Persons in all Degrees of Life. . . .

The publication of the *Director* in 1754 completely established his reputation and future fame. At that time English furniture was being copied and variously imitated in Europe as well as in North America and other English colonies, and the term Chippendale is used as the universal description for all specimens of what is called the 'Director' period. Such fame also brought problems in its wake. Many unjustified claims have been made that all Director pieces came from Chippendale's workshop when it is obvious that no single establishment could have been responsible for them. At the same time these claims demonstrate the sheer voracity with which his designs were seized upon, not only by the general public, but by his colleagues in London and in due course all over Britain. It is no wonder that Chippendale has been described as the 'high priest of mahogany'.

The two Thomas Chippendales

All we know of his life is confined to entries in parish records of baptism, marriage and burial, a few references in newspapers, a handful of letters and bills and other business papers. In spite of his professional success, he seems to have made little personal mark on his time. There is not even a portrait to throw any light on him.

He was a Yorkshireman born at Otley in 1718, the son of a joiner. There is nothing further recorded until the parish register states that on 19 May 1748 he was married to Catherine Redshaw at St George's Chapel, Hyde Park, London. It would be of the greatest interest to know how those first thirty vital years had been filled – presumably he worked with his father. We do not

Mahogany ladder-back chair.

know for certain how he made the move to London; almost certainly some form of sponsorship would have been necessary. Suitable patrons were available in Yorkshire, but once again we draw a complete blank concerning any record of direct assistance. Today near the junction of St Martin's Lane and Long Acre a plaque commemorates the site of Chippendale's last workshop. The London rate books tell us that he was previously in Conduit Court, Long Acre, from 1749 to 1752 and then in Somerset Court, Strand. In the middle of the eighteenth century that quarter of London was the centre of the furniture industry. In the following year Chippendale moved to 60 and 61 St Martin's Lane where he lived and worked for the rest of his life. The only real clue to the size of his business we owe to the fact that he was careful to insure his premises against fire. This was fortunate for a report in the *Gentleman's Magazine* of 5 April 1755 tells

Chippendale plain upholstered mahogany dining chair.

Chippendale period mahogany travelling secretaire. It contains a number of secret compartments and the pedestal is detachable.

us that a blaze at his workshop destroyed the benches of twenty-two workmen.

London was the principal centre of European furniture making and it was the London cabinet makers who set the fashion for the whole of Britain. Their position was strengthened by the great trading operations of the Port of London which ensured them a supply of the finest timbers. It was a competitive market and one of the largest workshops was that of George Seddon. No-one knows exactly where it was but a German visiting London in 1786 recorded that Seddon employed four hundred craftsmen. There is no doubt that Chippendale's *Director*, rather unfairly, tended to obscure the excellent work of some of his contemporaries. But it also stimulated fine cabinet work throughout the country. It ran to three editions and all its designs were in the latest fashion – even that old favourite the claw-and-ball foot was left out, presumably because it was outmoded – and its success was established beyond any doubt when other cabinet makers began to produce volumes of their own designs.

In the year of the publication of his *Director* Chippendale took James Rannie into his business. Very little is known of Rannie's career, but he died in 1766 and the Public Advertiser carried a notification of:

the entire genuine and valuable stock in trade of Mr Chippendale and his late partner Mr. Rannie, deceased, cabinet makers and upholsterers.

Five years later Chippendale took Thomas Haig into partnership who, it is believed, once acted as book-keeper to James Rannie. Accounts for furnishing at Harewood House and for David Garrick's home in the Adelphi are made out to Chippendale, Haig & Co, and it is very likely that Thomas Haig dealt more with the administrative side of the business. Chippendale had eleven children and when he died in 1779 his eldest son, also Thomas, carried on in partnership with Haig until 1796.

Thomas Chippendale the younger was clearly a man of artistic talent for he was, like his father, a member of the Society of Arts and even exhibited five pictures at the Royal Academy. He became bankrupt in 1804 and his stock of 'beautiful cabinet work of the first class' was dispersed. It did not prove a setback for long. He returned to business and shortly afterwards was again producing fine furniture for some of the finest houses in the land. His work holds particular interest in that it shows the transition from furniture of the late eighteenth century to that of the Regency and there is a fine collection that illustrates this at Stourhead in Wiltshire. His skill with the pencil enabled him when he visited Paris to return with a sketch book of drawings of Empire furniture and ornaments. He died in 1822.

Mahogany chair by Thomas Chippendale the younger. Early 19th century.

The Rococo, the Chinese and the Gothic

The principal contribution of Chippendale the elder was less to the invention of new furniture than to development and style. His work falls into three categories: the Rococo, the Chinese and the Gothic.

Chippendale commode showing French influence.

The Rococo style was entirely French in origin and it was Chippendale who anglicised it. The word comes from 'rocaille', which means rock-work. The style has a lively and sensual vigour, very unlike the heavy magnificence of the Baroque – an asymmetrical freedom of 'C' scrolls, double 'C' scrolls and swirling curves that resemble the breakers of the sea curling on some rocky shore.

In England, at first, the Rococo was not well received. Many architects, for example, were either unimpressed or even slightly alarmed by it. The silversmiths appear to have been among the first to react to its possibilities and some fine silver was produced; Huguenot craftsmen were naturally prepared to welcome the new style from France. In cabinet work the carvers and gilders led the way in taking advantage of the new ideas and Rococo then rapidly found its way into furniture design.

Chippendale himself used the 'C' scrolls, with flowers, foliage, shells and rocks in ornament. He also used birds and other figures to great advantage, and sometimes with humorous effect.

In the middle of the eighteenth century there was a revival of Oriental taste; many of the fashionable houses of the period boasted a Chinese room. Indeed, an advertisement in the London *Evening Post* of 8 January 1754 indicates that the taste for walls decorated in the Oriental style was quite extensive – and that one patentee was preparing to cash in on it:

BY THE KING'S PATENT
The new invented paper-hangings for ornamenting of rooms, Screens, &c., are to be had, by the Patentee's direction, of Thomas Vincent, Stationer, next door to the Wax-work in Fleet Street.

NOTE. – These new invented paper hangings in Beauty, Neatness and Cheapness infinitely surpass anything of the like nature hitherto made use of; being not distinguishable from rich India paper, and the same being beautifully coloured in pencil work and gilt.

Any person who imitates the said paper contrary to his Majesty's said Patent, granted for 14 years from 22nd August 1753, will be prosecuted.

Hanging shelves from the 'Director'.

The Oriental revival naturally created a market for furniture and Chippendale met the demand with his own special designs. He achieved what was perhaps his most successful effect of Chinoiserie in his superb mirrors – in the carved and gilt girandoles and pier glasses ornately decorated with scrolls which often bear bold Oriental motifs. Many of the mirrors of the period, however – not only those attributable to Chippendale – carry such features as pagodas, Chinese figures and long-tailed birds; occasionally some have Chinese paintings behind the glass, the work of Chinese artists.

In 1747 Horace Walpole purchased a house at Strawberry Hill and, with great enthusiasm he transformed it into the most famous Gothic villa in the world. The Gothic tracery, with its arcading, crockets and pointed windows, has a lightness and distinction all its own and makes 'Strawberry Hill Gothic' unique. It infuriated students of the medieval, but this fashion for filigree could hardly have been a more fitting companion for the scrolls of Rococo; and it had a great effect on those who were commissioning or buying furniture or, like Chippendale, designing and making it.

Mahogany side table in Gothic style, based on a 'Director' design.

Chippendale chairs

Chippendale designed a great many chairs, and these varied greatly in the amount of carving they carried. Before Chippendale the heavier cabriole usually had a deep scroll carved on the knee, rather in the fashion of ram's horns, and a moulding on the edge of the leg. Chippendale lightened these features, giving the cabriole a cleaner sweep; yet never for a moment did he cut back on the timber at the knee and the foot as this might have made them appear attenuated. He re-introduced the H-shaped stretchers on many designs and favoured the square leg with chamfered inside edges. Some of his vase-shaped splats were intricately cut with curves yet still remained essentially plain; and the arms of his open armchairs often made an elegant sweep of the practical curve for elbow and forearm, terminating in an underscroll or patera to provide a comfortable terminal for the hand and fingers.

In general, even in simple country furniture the emphasis was on comfort. In the wheel and stickback chair the elm seat was frequently being adzed in order to achieve a saddle effect that would make a cushion unnecessary. The open armchairs with upholstered seat and back that Chippendale clearly enjoyed are again a joy to sit in; they were broad enough in the seat to accommodate the eighteenth-century skirt or the amply filled breeches of the 'four bottle men' who, more often than not, began the day with beef steak for breakfast.

Dining chairs with square legs frequently carry pierced brackets where the leg joins the seat; the shaped and pierced vase splat – and the ample 'cupid's bow' cresting rail with back supports curving outwards to meet it – could either be left plain or could be richly carved with acanthus leaves or ribbons. The 'ribband-

Mahogany 'ribband-back' chair with the splat formed by scrolls and interlaced ribbons.

back' chairs could also take decoration to extremes with heavily carved legs of cabriole form terminating in a scrolled foot and the splat a mass of deeply carved puckered ribbon – which produced a sense of the Rococo that is rather more French than English. In fact Chippendale did design 'French' chairs. He visited France in 1768 and the following year he was fined when importing unfinished French furniture, which no doubt he was intending to complete in his workshop. At any rate, he failed to declare sixty French chair frames at their full value. The *Director* carries designs for 'French' upholstered armchairs with carved and scrolled frames intended for gilding.

His 'Chinese' chairs owe most of their Oriental taste to their pierced legs and fret backs. Occasionally the stretchers and seat

Chinese Chippendale chair in the 'Director'.

79

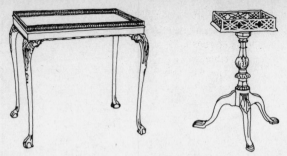

(Left) Chippendale period tea table c. 1760 with fret gallery and finely carved acanthus knees. (Right) Mahogany tea kettle stand.

rails would be fret cut in addition to the front legs, and fret mouldings were also used. Fret carving was used by Chippendale on his tea tables or, as he described them, 'china tables'. These tables carried a low fret gallery around the edge, and fret cut brackets between the legs and table top. Mahogany breakfast tables also carried frets below and, where an undershelf was present, the entire shelf was enclosed with frets and doors. At first, when frets were cut out of a single layer of wood, they were obviously not very strong and rather easily broken. So the practice began of gluing three even thinner layers together, with the grain of the middle layer running across the grain of the outer layers; and what was probably the earliest form of plywood made its appearance.

Mahogany breakfast table.

Chippendale's designs covered a very wide range of furniture and the forms of decoration he used were almost equally varied. His side tables in the Gothic taste – which superseded the massive side tables and console tables of William Kent – often dis-

Artist's table in mahogany with lattice-work frieze and cluster column legs, c. 1755.

played, as indeed did other pieces in his Gothic style, legs cut to form a 'cluster column' effect. Superb breakfront bookcases were supplied by Chippendale with fine mouldings and broken pediments of scroll swan neck form. In Chippendale's day what we now call a bureau bookcase was known as a 'desk and book-case', and one of the best-known examples attributed to him, which features relief carving of the highest quality, is the 'violin' mahogany bureau bookcase made about 1760 which is in the col-lection of the Earl of Pembroke at Wilton House, Wiltshire. Some of Chippendale's magnificent chests of drawers show the use of the serpentine curve at its best, while some of his com-modes clearly took their inspiration from French originals. The furniture produced by Chippendale – and that of other makers of what is called the 'Chippendale Period' – was not of course con-fined to those pieces illustrated in his *Director*. In fact he produced furniture to suit the taste of his patrons and the requirements of the day and so there is very little to which he did not turn his hand.

The impact of the *Director* rolled on for decades, but in fashionable London it was rapidly outdated by the rise of the Neo-Classical movement and it is at this time that we begin to associate the name of Robert Adam with that of Thomas Chip-pendale.

6
Robert Adam and Neo-Classicism

A family of architects

Robert Adam (1728–1792), the architect and furniture designer, was himself the son of an architect, William Adam, who had a flourishing practice in Scotland. Robert began his training with his father and it was then decided that he should visit Southern Europe to complete his studies and to learn something of Classical architecture. It was a decision that had far-reaching effects, not only on his own career but on the whole course of English design.

He arrived in Italy in 1754 at a moment when the Italians were in the throes of one of their periodic obsessions with their own past; the Bourbon king of Naples was an amateur of archaeology and a number of Roman sites were rediscovered during his reign. Whether or not Adam was infected by the general excitement, he was certainly enthralled by the relics and monuments of the ancient world – by the massive dignity of Roman building and by its decoration; by the paintings and stuccos, the statues and reliefs in temples, baths and villas. He admired the 'grotesques' in the Vatican and the Villa Madama; and the newly discovered statue of Antinous in the Capitol. In 1755 he visited Tivoli and the Villa of Hadrian where he saw the celebrated mosaic of doves drinking from a fountain; and in the same year he went south to Naples. He toured Pompeii – luckily missing an eruption of Vesuvius which occurred at about that time – and Herculaneum, which was still being excavated.

In 1757 he travelled to Dalmatia where he saw the magnificent Palace of Diocletian at Spalato (now Split). It was this palace which inspired the Adelphi buildings in London and the visit to Spalato therefore had an important influence on his career. It also nearly put an end to it. While he was drawing the massive granite columns and the Corinthian capitals of the peristyle – the main courtyard of the palace – he was arrested as a spy. But once again he was lucky; the commander of the garrison was a fellow

Scot, a Jacobite general called Robert Graeme and thanks to him, Adam was released.

He arrived in England in 1758, his notebooks filled with beautiful drawings; but in spite of the careful study he had made of his models, the designs he produced had an originality and distinction that were all his own and he found the fashionable world in a mood to appreciate them. In the England of the Augustan age, Neo-Classicism was exactly suited to the spirit of the times.

Sir John Soane, the architect of the Bank of England, was quick to see the importance and variety of Adam's work. After Adam's death Soane purchased more than nine thousand of his original drawings, a large proportion of which are of furniture. These can still be seen at the Soane Museum in London. Most of the designs take the form of primary sketches and ideas; later finished drawings were most likely sent to individual cabinet makers in the usual manner. Some years later, in 1812, Sir John Soane delivered a lecture in which he stated:

> The light and elegant ornaments, the varied compartments in the ceilings of Mr Adam, imitated from Ancient Works in the Baths and Villas of the Romans were soon applied in designs of chairs, tables, carpets and in every other species of furniture. To Mr. Adam's taste in the ornament of his buildings and furniture we stand indebted, inasmuch as manufacturers of every kind felt, as it were, the electric power of this revolution in art.

After his return from the Continent Robert Adam set up an architectural practice of his own in London taking his three brothers, James, John and William, into the firm; and within a decade he had established his reputation. Some years later, in 1778, Robert and James Adam published the results of the great changes they had wrought in architecture and interior design in a folio volume of engravings entitled *The Works in Architecture of Robert and James Adam*, and here we come across the following statement:

> we have not only met with the approbation of our employers, but even with the imitation of other artists, to such a degree, as in some measure to have brought about, in this country, a kind of revolution . . .

Robert Adam was given the title, with Sir William Chambers, of Joint Architect to His Majesty's Works. It was Sir William

Chambers, incidentally, who stimulated the popularity of the Oriental taste in the middle of the eighteenth century with his *Designs for Chinese Buildings, Furniture, Dresses etc.* which, based on a visit he himself had made to China, was published in 1757.

There are a number of major examples of Adam's Neo-Classical work: among them are Harewood House and Nostell Priory in Yorkshire, Osterley Park and Syon House in Middlesex, Kedleston in Derbyshire, Saltram House in Devonshire and Apsley House and several other fine houses in London. His architectural work falls rather conveniently into two main periods: the first from 1760–1770 and the second 1770–1780 when a sophistication had taken over from his earlier boldness. Many critics have found fault with the later designs, judging the extreme delicacy to be trivial and lacking in dignity. The ever critical Horace Walpole describes them as 'snippets of embroidery and gingerbread'.

Adam and Chippendale

Adam's furniture also evolved in phases but the divisions between them are less distinct, so that a close study of his work is required if one is to differentiate clearly between them. Many of the earlier designs were based upon well-tried Georgian examples, although the carved ornament of such pieces is distinctly Classical. In his hands scrolls of foliage become more formal, and we already see his celebrated honeysuckle and carved paterae appearing.

Adam believed that the interior design and furnishing of a room should add up to one harmonious whole and he used the same ornamental motifs in carpets, ceilings, chimney pieces, overdoors, friezes and furniture: sphinxes, griffins, vases, urns, formal leaves, female figures, goats' and rams' head masks, satyrs' heads, anthemion (honeysuckle), festoons of flowers or husks, paterae and medallions. Thomas Chippendale himself was swift to see the possibilities of the new fashion – and this was

Motifs much favoured by Adam: ram's head, honeysuckle and griffin.

a period that was to bring about much closer working between the interior designer and the cabinet maker.

It is highly unlikely that all of the furniture of Adam's style to be found in Adam houses was the work of the architect himself. A number of superb craftsmen worked for Adam. Thomas Chippendale, John Linnell, Thomas Cobb, William France, Samuel Norman, William Beckwith and Ince and Mayhew were outstanding among them. But craftsmen of their calibre were quite capable, after discussions with the architect, of carrying through some of the designs themselves. Also, although Adam appears to have supplied designs for all the furniture that was to line the walls of his rooms, such as side tables, pier glasses, cabinets, commodes and sideboards, the remaining furniture required by the owner of the house was ordered from the cabinet makers themselves, who would set out to complement the overall taste and design.

It says much for the English craftsmen that they could turn so readily to new ideas and execute, with outstanding skill, forms of decoration either entirely new or perhaps not in use for a generation or more. Marquetry, for example, had long been neglected but now it was revived with a remarkable degree of smoothness and delicacy. The added advantage given to work of this kind was the large number of new timbers of great beauty becoming available. Tulipwood, the hard and heavy timber that frequently shaded itself from yellow to red in variegated stripes and was imported from Brazil in the second half of the eighteenth century, was often employed as a cross-banded veneer and was favoured by Chippendale. The yellow satinwood, plain or richly figured, was used considerably as a veneer after 1765, although it was not often used in the solid for furniture construction. The so-called harewood was normally sycamore or maple stained with oxide of iron. These timbers, and also the use of painted decoration, created furniture that was light and bright and in complete harmony with its surroundings.

For his painted furniture Adam tended to choose beech, on which paint could be directly applied. Beech frames could also be easily gilded. He liked to apply painted decoration to fine veneers, usually in the form of festoons and medallions. He had designs painted on copper panels and even on paper, that were cut out to any required shape. By the end of the eighteenth century the art of marquetry, which had been so briefly yet brilliantly revived, had once more slipped from fashion; painted decoration on furniture had taken its place.

Painted wood candlestand designed by Robert Adam, c. 1772.

The ormolu mounts which were so particularly attractive when set against the darker timbers were initially imported from France. The term 'ormolu' is used to describe bronze or brass which has been chased or chiselled and then coated with an amalgam of gold and mercury and fired, causing the mercury to pass off as vapour and the gold to adhere to the metal. This method is now illegal as an industrial process, for the vapour given off is lethal. In 1762 the need to import ormolu from France lessened as the great industrialist Matthew Boulton and his partner James Watt opened their factory at Soho near Birmingham and began to produce ormolu of very high quality. A contemporary letter refers to Matthew Boulton as being '. . . very desirous of cultivating Mr. Adam's taste in his productions'. A further important development in the embellishment of furniture occurred in 1777 when Samuel Bellamy and John Marsten, Birmingham brass founders, patented a method of stamping designs on metal that could be applied to furniture. It made possible the development of brass handles and knobs of all kinds, including the lion ring handle that was to become so popular by the beginning of the nineteenth century.

It was not only English craftsmen who contributed to the success of the Adam brothers. They recruited talent from the Continent as well and one of their most notable employees was the Swiss artist Angelica Kauffmann (1741–1807) who was elected to the Royal Academy in 1768. She painted ceilings and mural de-

An Adam pedestal typical of Neo-Classical design.

corations for many of Adam's houses – and her work, incidentally, is almost certainly the inspiration for the painted medallions on much of the furniture of the period. She married Antonio Zucchi (1726–1795), a Venetian artist who also painted for the Adam brothers and in 1757 had joined Robert Adam on his journey through Italy and Dalmatia. Another Continental artist who came to England at Adam's request was Michele Pergolesi; he painted panels, mainly in the Etruscan and the Grotesque styles.

Some notable Neo-Classical furniture

In the same way that a chair in the French style had been created by Chippendale, so a 'French Adam' chair developed. It appeared in the mid-1770's with cabriole legs and scroll feet, fine upholstery and the gentle curves associated with the work of Adam. There were also French Adam chairs with fluted tapered legs. He brought the cane seat back into favour and round and oval backs; but heart shapes and shields were also fashionable. The Grecian lyre was sometimes used as a motif but this was to come into greater prominence in the Regency period.

Adam chair in the French manner.

The inventory of Appuldurcombe House – now a ruin – on the Isle of Wight provides good evidence of the possibility that a house could be completely furnished in the Adam style by Chippendale, although Adam himself had no connection with it. One set of chairs from Appuldurcombe were inset with Wedgwood medallions – demonstrating once again how many of the arts had been affected by the Neo-Classical influence.

From the accounts of 1773 of Harewood House we find Chippendale's entry for the famous 'Diana and Minerva' commode:

> A very large rich commode with exceeding fine Antique Ornaments curiously inlaid with various fine woods. Drawers at each end and enclosed with foldg: Doors with Diana and Minerva and their Emblems curiously Inlaid and Engraved, a Cupboard in the middle part with a Cove Door, a Dressing Drawer in the Top part, the whole Elegantly Executed and Varnished, with many wrought Brass Antique Ornaments finely finished.

This magnificent piece – for which he charged £86 – was the most expensive item of cased furniture Chippendale ever made. The cove door referred to in the bill is the concave lunette in the bottom centre portion of the commode. The pilasters and feet are mounted in ormolu and the figures of goddesses on the doors are carried out in coloured woods and ivory on a groundwork of ebony.

The japanned bedroom furniture at Nostell Priory also displays Chippendale's mastery of materials and design. Indeed, the English furniture of this period is as superb as any made by contemporary French craftsmen.

Another most striking example of Adam furniture design to be found at Harewood House is the famous rosewood sideboard. It too was probably supplied by Chippendale, sometime between 1770 and 1775. It bears much of the ornament most favoured by Adam – anthemion, paterae, masks and so on – mounted in ormolu. The sideboard table is flanked by separate pedestals surmounted by well-proportioned urns – which are wine coolers; it was Adam, in fact, who introduced pedestals for storing dining room articles. A separate wine cooler completes the sideboard suite. There are many critics who, while not disputing the superb quality of the craftsmanship, contend that the sideboard is of little practical use until the table, urns and pedestals are all combined into one unit and indeed, this was later to become common practice.

Rosewood sideboard table with pedestals, urns and wine cooler, mounted in ormolu in the Neo-Classical style. Attributed to Chippendale, c. 1770–1775.

It has to be admitted that Robert Adam, while he produced some of the finest furniture this country has ever seen, designed it primarily for display in the 'state' rooms of a house and that use and comfort were secondary considerations. Some of his designs have also been criticised for a certain effeminacy; an example is the state bed made for Osterley Park which resembled a Classical temple, complete with columns and a dome festooned with artificial flowers. Horace Walpole, never a tolerant man, was affronted by it. 'What would Vitruvius have thought', he asked, 'of a dome decorated by a milliner?'

7

Other Eighteenth-Century Makers and Designers

Timbers

The rare and beautiful timbers that had been used in English furniture since Elizabethan times were a by-product of Britain's vast sea power. All over the world her navies guarded the trade routes and her merchantmen 'followed the Flag'. With the merchantmen went soldiers – to America to fight the colonists; convicts – to Captain Cook's new settlement in Botany Bay; explorers, missionaries, administrators, remittance men – even slaves. But in the eighteenth century many a ship's complement also included a cartographer to chart the new territories, a botanist in search of new food crops and flowers and trees, a geologist to look for precious stones and valuable minerals. As more of the world was discovered and explored, English horizons widened and new ideas and new materials began to have their effect on design.

In the first half of the eighteenth century the *London Tradesman* was quoting the woods then available in the yards of the London timber merchants. They were:

> Furnished with Deal from Norway; with Oak and Wainscot from Sweden; and some from the Counties of England; with Mahogany from Jamaica; with Walnut-Tree from Spain.

The deal that came from the Baltic shipyards was used in the main by the cabinet maker to provide the carcase for his veneers, but as the century moved into its second half the red deal from North America was increasingly employed for this purpose. The best of the imported oak was used for drawer linings, and rosewood, originally used as a veneer, was now found to be practicable in the solid. Rosewood was first imported from the West Indies then later from the East and Brazil. It is a very satisfying, heavy, dark timber with red-brown streaks and occasional black markings. It gets its name from the fragrance arising from the timber when it is sawn. Another variety of rosewood is referred to as padouk, again a heavy timber with considerable variety in coloration and frequently having a distinct red appearance. It was brought to England from Burma and the Andaman Islands. Examples of furniture – most of them chairs – executed in solid padouk are rare and they tend to be of exceptional quality. The yellow-coloured satinwood was imported from the West Indies and Guiana from about 1760, and from the East Indies from about 1770. One of the most popular woods of the period, it was used in the solid as well as for veneering and inlaying.

In the late eighteenth century other new and exotic timbers provided further choice for the cabinet maker. Calamander from Ceylon, in reds and browns, thuya from Africa, amboyna from the West Indies and the well-known coromandel from India were now available. Purple wood, zebra wood, kingwood and tulipwood – all exciting contrasting timbers imported from Brazil – were used to provide either decorative bandings or veneers. Red cedar from North America was used for drawer linings. Not all the imported timbers were so successful: after about 1770 the West Indian wood known as fustic caught the designer's and craftsman's eye because of its interesting yellow coloration, but it was swiftly abandoned when it was discovered that the colour faded to a lack-lustre brown.

For japanning, gilding, painting and gesso work, cheaper native timbers could be used. Beech was a favourite for chair frames but it is also found in case furniture together with deal, pearwood and lime. There were other uses too for local timbers; chestnut and birch could sometimes resemble satinwood; sycamore was popular as a veneer and yew was highly prized by some individual craftsmen. Ebony had been imported for some two hundred years and as the demand for it increased, it was discovered that certain close-grained timbers such as willow or pear could be stained to create an 'ebonised' effect and were therefore used for the very fine lines of inlay known as stringing.

Country craftsmen

In the countryside most craftsmen also used local timbers; and in remoter country areas much of the furniture was still made to traditional designs. Horace Walpole, a mine of information as usual, mentions a friend who:

> picked up a whole cloisterful of old chairs in Herefordshire. He bought them one by one, here and there in farm houses for three and sixpence and a crown apiece. They are of wood, the

seats triangular, the backs, arms and legs loaded with turnery. A thousand to one but there are plenty up and down Cheshire too.

The upper classes who had houses in the country now bought most of their furniture in London while middle-class people who lived in the provinces were usually supplied by the highly competent cabinet makers in provincial towns. Some cheap furniture was also transported from London in vessels trading with coastal ports; in the countryside itself, transportation was a more arduous business. In April 1793 Parson Woodforde records:

> About two o'clock this Afternoon two men of Sudbury's at Norwich came with my Sideboard and a large New Mahogany Cellaret bought of Sudbury, brought on the Men's Shoulders all the way and very safe.

It is unfortunate that so little is recorded of the provincial cabinet makers; it is no doubt due to the fact that they created so little furniture that was personally distinctive to them. The eighteenth-century poll books often give the names of two or three cabinet makers in a market town, but unless an example is found bearing perhaps a trade label or a written inscription on the under side of a bottom board of a drawer, their life's work is destined to be anonymous. In recent years it has become clear that the range of skills possessed by these cabinet makers and of the furniture they made was far wider than previously thought. Increasing interest in local history studies will certainly produce further welcome information in this field.

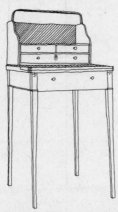

A cheveret, or writing table with detachable book trough.

The Gillow family firm

One of the firms of provincial craftsmen to achieve distinction was that established by the Gillow family of Lancaster. The trade papers of this great family business are probably the most complete in existence and have now been saved for the nation. The founder of the firm was Robert Gillow who started business as a joiner in Lancaster. His joiner's shop developed rapidly into a high-class furniture-making business, but he was also a general trader. He traded with the West Indies, was a licensed dealer in rum, an undertaker, a jobbing carpenter and a spirit merchant as well as being a furniture maker.

Inlaid oval tea caddy, bearing the stamp of Gillows.

About 1740 Robert Gillow began shipping furniture to London. He did not regard himself as a great designer any more than did his son Richard who became his partner in 1757. Their workmanship was of true excellence and in due course Gillows opened a branch in London – an event characteristically described in the Gillow ledger as 'the adventure to London'. This London branch first appears as Gillow & Barton, and it was established outside the main London cabinet-making areas of St Martin's Lane and Covent Garden.

Richard Gillow, a full partner at the age of twenty-three, made furniture of the first order, not only for the nobility but even for royalty. He had great confidence in himself and in his work. There is a story that once, when showing a table that was priced at eighty guineas to a nobleman, his lordship was heard to exclaim: 'It's a devil of a price.' 'It's a devil of a table,' replied Richard Gillow, and with that the sale was sealed. As an inventor he was responsible for the first billiard table and also patented the telescopic dining table. Much of his work has been confused with that of Hepplewhite and Sheraton, but fortunately the firm's case furniture was often sensibly stamped with the name 'Gillows' or 'Gillows, Lancaster'. This stamped signature appears most frequently on drawer edges – a practice adopted by many makers during the nineteenth century.

Among the records of the firm of Gillow there is an entry which reads: 'Captain Davenport, a desk'. It is probable that this was the first desk of its type that was ever made and that it was named after the customer who commissioned it. Basically, the Davenport desk is a case of drawers surmounted by a sloping writing top with locker beneath. Those of the very early nineteenth century are extremely elegant, usually made either of solid mahogany or veneered in rosewood. Desks of this type have many slight variations in design, usually involving the number and positioning of cupboards, drawers, slides etc. Pierced brass galleries are a common feature in the design, and so is satinwood inlay; they also usually have short tapered feet mounted on brass castors.

There is a great deal of difference between the examples mentioned above and those of the Victorian era. The Victorians, like their Regency predecessors, were great letter writers, and a slightly larger design, more typical of the nineteenth century, rapidly evolved. It remained in the form of a sloping writing top with locker and with drawers and cupboards below; but whereas early examples have a tall box-like construction not unlike the later Wellington chest, the Victorians continued the locker writing top beyond the drawer fronts and supported the protruding ends upon pillar supports of various designs. A great many of the Victorian Davenports were veneered in walnut, and fine examples of Davenport desks are among the most attractive pieces of writing furniture to exist in the early nineteenth century.

Davenport writing desk showing the clean lines of the earlier examples.

Hepplewhite

For many people the style of George Hepplewhite typifies all that is best in eighteenth-century English cabinet making; and yet not a single piece of his furniture – or that of his workshop – has ever been positively identified. Nor is much known of his life; although it has been suggested that he was apprenticed to Gillow of Lancaster, all we know for certain is that he had a business in Redcross Street, Cripplegate, London. No record remains of his work there, however, and his name is only well known to us because of the publication of his book, *The Cabinet Maker and Upholsterer's Guide*, which appeared in 1788, two years after his death. It was published by his widow Alice, who carried on the business. A second edition came out in the following year and a third in 1794. It contains nearly three hundred designs, many of them adaptations of originals by Adam and all distinguished by the characteristic lightness and elegance, unencumbered by unnecessary ornament, that we have come to associate with the name of Hepplewhite.

Mahogany 'shield back' chair with satinwood inlay. Based on a design in Hepplewhite's 'Guide'.

One of the most celebrated of his chair designs is the shield back supported entirely by the upright projections of the back legs, the base of the shield making no contact at all with the seat or back seat rail. He favoured fluted legs, carved wheat-ears, rosettes, carved paterae, festoons of drapery, pendant husks, classical urns and other decorations in the Neo-Classical taste. He also used the Prince of Wales feathers. His chair legs tend to be of square section with a slight taper down to plinth feet, the tapering often taking place on the inside of the leg. His shield back chairs, however, were probably a popularisation of an existing form; and chairs with an oval or heart-shaped back, which were produced in some numbers in this period, cannot be looked upon as his invention even though today they are often termed 'Hepplewhite'.

Tambour fronts were used in some Hepplewhite pieces and so were bow fronts, his small bow-fronted sideboards being particularly successful. He also designed bow-front and serpentine-front chests of drawers which were made with the drawer fronts in mahogany veneered on pine. The same technique was prescribed for straight-fronted chests but there are also examples in solid mahogany. Hepplewhite's designs emphasise the grace of the period not only in line and proportion but also in such detail as the mahogany glazing bars on the doors of glass-fronted cabinets.

A serpentine-front chest of graduated drawers with brushing slide.

His sofas differ markedly from those designed by Adam; but then fashions in deportment had changed. In the mid-century it had been correct – in company at any rate – to sit with the back straight and to avoid what Lord Chesterfield called 'odd motions, strange postures and ungenteel carriage'. Adam's sofas are clearly intended for the disciples of Lord Chesterfield. But by the nineties manners and deportment had become more relaxed. Ease and grace were now as essential in behaviour and bearing as they were in women's clothes. Hepplewhite designed sofas with deeper seats in which the sitter could take his ease.

His style is at once rational and refined; the secretaire cabinet is a splendid example of elegance and ingenuity: the top drawer in the chest base can be pulled out and then its front lowered to form a surface for writing; the glazed upper parts are often capped with vase-shaped pediments or urns. A strong French influence is also to be found in the curving lines of many of his designs – particularly in his open armchairs with upholstered seats and backs, and small window seats. This kind of furniture is referred to as 'French Hepplewhite' and is again an indication of the powerful French influence on English taste – which had at no time completely disappeared since the Restoration.

Hepplewhite period painted armchair, c. 1770.

Hepplewhite's book was the most important publication of furniture designs to make its appearance since Chippendale's *Director*, and his accent on the creation of ever lighter furniture was welcomed. Perhaps the most distinctive feature of Hepplewhite design, apart from the continuing influence of French Rococo, is the chest of drawers or cabinet where the apron of the base is cut to produce a drooping continuous curve running on into outward splay feet. George Hepplewhite was also the first cabinet maker to illustrate a Pembroke table in his book of designs. It was an item of furniture that was in great demand in the late eighteenth century, and it particularly attracted the eye of Thomas Sheraton.

Other eighteenth-century craftsmen

In an age which fostered talent as successfully as the eighteenth century there must have been many craftsmen whose names are now forgotten; there are also a number whose work as cabinet makers, designers, upholsterers and specialists of one kind or another made important contributions to English furniture and decoration during this period. Their names are in alphabetical order.

Samuel Beckwith supplied furniture for Buckingham Palace and was in partnership with William France.

John Bradburn, a cabinet maker who was employed by Vile and Cobb and supplied furniture to the royal household. He was a specialist in carving and cabinet maker to the Crown in partnership with William France.

William Bradshaw, an important furniture maker of the mid-eighteenth century whose name appears in the accounts for furnishing Longford Castle, Wiltshire and who made furniture at Holkham, Norfolk. One of the subscribers to Chippendale's *Director* in 1754 is listed as William Bradshaw Esq. and it is very likely that the reference is to this cabinet maker.

George Brookshaw was employed on furnishings at Carlton House and in 1783 provided for the Prince of Wales an 'elegant commode highly finished with a basket of flowers painted in the front and sprays of jasmine all over the top, and ditto on the front, the body with carved and gilt mouldings and legs'.

Robert Campbell made a major contribution to the furnishing of Carlton House and excellent examples of late eighteenth-century furniture in the royal collections have been attributed to him.

John Cobb (d. 1778), cabinet maker and upholsterer at St Martin's Lane and partner of William Vile. He carried out important work for George III and supplied furniture to many major houses; he created a considerable personal fortune.

Edward Edwards (1738–1806) worked in the shop of William Hallett where he drew patterns for furniture. Later he taught drawing to 'several young men who either aimed to be artists or to qualify themselves to be cabinet or ornamental furniture makers'. He was elected Associate of the Royal Academy in 1775 and was later designing furniture for Horace Walpole at Strawberry Hill.

William France appears among the list of tradesmen patronised by Royalty in 1765, and he was responsible for most of the furniture at Kenwood. The contents of Kenwood have since been dispersed. France succeeded William Vile as cabinet maker to the Crown in 1764.

John Gumley had a looking-glass shop in the Strand. It was described by Steele in 1715 as 'A place where people may go and be very well entertained, whether they have or have not good taste ... it is not in the power of any Potentate in Europe to have so beautiful a mirror as he may purchase here for a trifle'. A gilt slip bearing the name Gumley appears on a mirror at Hampton Court Palace.

W. and J. Halfpenny were architects and designers of furniture who were important in fostering the Oriental taste in England. Between 1750 and 1752 William Halfpenny and his son John set about publishing in parts their designs for Chinese temples together with designs for a few chairs and mirrors. They also produced 'rural architecture in the Chinese taste'. Their furniture designs might well be termed incongruous.

William Hallett (1707–1781). During the second quarter of the eighteenth century William Hallett was one of the most fashionable furniture makers of the day. He was employed by the Earl of Leicester, Lord Folkestone and the Earl of Pembroke. When the home of the Duke of Chandos, Cannons, near Edgware, was sold the estate was purchased by Hallett who built for himself a fine house on the site of the old one.

Frances Herve, another of the late eighteenth-century craftsmen who carried out work at Carlton House for the Prince of Wales and who supplied nearly £3,000 worth of furniture to the house on the direction of Henry Holland the architect and designer. He was basically employed as a chair maker with his workshop in Lower John Street, Tottenham Court Road. Much of his work owes a great deal to French influence, and his workshop continued until the end of the eighteenth century. In the Victoria and Albert Museum there is a set of library steps carrying Herve's label.

John Hodson was a cabinet maker with a looking glass and cabinet warehouse in Frith Street, Soho, from 1724 to 1744. He specialised in japanned work and also supplied furniture for the Duke of Atholl and for Lord Monson.

Robert Hodson, also of Frith Street and well known for his letter to Sir Edward de Bouverie where he describes an unusually elaborate fitted bureau he has made for Sir Edward, and comments that he had placed upon it 'strong brass wheels or casters that you may more easily move it to the fire'.

Henry Holland (1746–1806), architect and furniture designer. He held the appointment of Architect to the Prince of Wales and was responsible for enlarging Carlton House. The Prince of Wales, having come of age, had left what he regarded as the confining atmosphere of the Palace and proceeded to set up a home in his own right, designed and furnished to his own choice. Some of the furniture designed by Holland for Carlton House is now at Buckingham Palace and a number of other fine pieces of furniture in mahogany and gilt are in the royal collections. From 1783 until 1806 Henry Holland was principal designer for the Prince. Many of his designs were in the Graeco-Roman manner; while Graeco-Roman styles are normally associated with the Regency period, it can be seen from the work for Carlton House that such designs were already well established in the late eighteenth century.

William Ince and John Mayhew. A major partnership among the eighteenth-century cabinet makers was Ince and Mayhew who rose to prominence after their publication of the *Universal System of Household Furniture* between 1759 and 1762, a folio edition of which was dedicated to the Duke of Marlborough who was Lord Chamberlain of His Majesty's Household. It is very probable that Chippendale and Ince and Mayhew were conscious of one another's intentions, and that something of a race developed for first publication between the *Universal System* and the third edition of the *Director*. A great many of the illustrations by Ince and Mayhew show marked similarities to those in the *Director*, and it is not overstating the situation to say that there are clear cases of plagiarism from Chippendale. Indeed Ince was one of the subscribers to the Chippendale volume. Ince and Mayhew worked from Broad Street, Golden Square, where they stated: '... every article in the several Branches treated of is executed on the most reasonable terms with the utmost neatness and punctuality'. Later this firm moved to an address off Carnaby Market. The authors' notes in their *Universal System* are in both French and English and demonstrate their ambitions towards the Continental market.

Gerreit Jensen. Although he was cabinet maker to the royal household, and his work covers a span from Charles II to the end of the reign of Queen Anne, little is known of his background. His major period of work was between 1680 and 1715. From royal inventories and accounts it is clear that much of Jensen's work was decorated very much in the style of the day – that is, with japan or marquetry – and that he favoured the use of ebony. Accounts in William III's reign show him as having supplied glass panels and mirrors for Hampton Court. Much of his fine furniture was also inlaid with metal. Among his accounts of 1699 to 1700 there is an entry that refers to the payment of a servant to 'pollish and whiten a Beuro inlaid with mettal'. Less elaborate furniture was supplied for Queen Anne; he is recorded as providing furniture for the Queen's drawing room at St James's to the sum of £450 consisting of stands, gilt tables and mirrors.

John Linnell, cabinet maker, carver and designer who died in 1786. A considerable collection of Linnell's drawings is held at the Victoria and Albert Museum; he was responsible for a great deal of important work ranging in style from the Rococo to the Neo-Classical. A magnificent bed in the Chinese manner at Osterley Park, previously regarded as the work of Thomas Chippendale, is now known to have been the work of Linnell.

Matthias Lock, a carver and designer working between 1740 and 1769. During this period he published eleven books of designs and was one of the earliest advocates of the English Rococo style. Two of the books were published in collaboration with H. Copland whose *New Book of Ornaments* which appeared in 1746 also demonstrates some of the earliest English Rococo.

Robert Manwaring, cabinet maker, chair maker and designer who published *The Cabinet and Chair Maker's Real Friend and Companion* in 1765. He asserted that his designs were 'calculated for all people in different stations of life'. His *Chair Maker's Guide* of 1762 later drew scant praise from Thomas Sheraton who said its content consisted only of 'what a boy may be taught in seven hours'.

Thomas Shearer, cabinet maker and designer. Much of his work is distinctive in character and was praised by Sheraton.

Charles Tatham (1772–1842), younger brother of Thomas, was yet another of the architects who exerted vast influence on furniture design in the late eighteenth and early nineteenth centuries. He was a pupil of Henry Holland who encouraged him to visit Italy where he spent some three years. While Henry Holland was engaged in the decoration and furnishing of Carlton House, Tatham sent him letters and drawings containing details of bronzes and other decorations including Egyptian antiquities on display in Rome. Tatham was clearly instrumental in giving impetus to the Grecian style.

Thomas Tatham (1763–1818), of the firm Marsh & Tatham,

supplied much of Holland's furniture and from 1795 he was principal cabinet maker to the Prince.

William Vile (d. 1767) was the partner of John Cobb. Together they were among the major furniture manufacturers employed early in the reign of George III. Carved pendants, wreaths and masks are characteristic of the enrichments he employed, and much of his design for larger items of furniture shows a distinct architectural sense of scale and ornament.

Sheraton

The new ease of manners, the simplicity and spontaneity that became fashionable towards the end of the eighteenth century, reflected a new spirit that was rising in the world. Rousseau had taught his readers to value the 'untutored impulse of the heart' and Ossian celebrated ravines and ruins; young ladies in simple muslin dresses took to walking in the woods, reading Cowper and meditating on the influence of nature. The clear outlines, realism and balance of the Augustan age were blurred in the dawn of romanticism.

Harlequin Pembroke table, with a box-like compartment fitted with drawers which can be concealed or raised at will by the use of counterweights. From a design in Sheraton's 'Drawing Book' of 1791–94.

The new taste brought changes to every aspect of life; restraint gave way to enthusiasm, the minuet to the waltz, sense to sensibility. Powdered heads and corsets went out of fashion at about the time the old king was put into a strait-waistcoat; the 'picturesque' began to dominate landscape gardening; architects *built* ruins; and in interiors, the formal vistas of furniture, carefully arranged for ceremony and display, were replaced by small groups of tables – tables in nests, tables for tea or for sewing, for cards or for breakfast – in keeping with the new feeling for relaxed elegance. By 1816 the fashion had spread into the country and in *Persuasion*, Jane Austen describes a visit to a country house, in Somerset:

> the old-fashioned square parlour, with a small carpet and shining floor, to which the present daughters of the house were gradually giving the proper air of confusion by a grand piano-forte and a harp, flower-stands and little tables placed in every direction.

Sheraton bonheur du jour.

Much of Thomas Sheraton's furniture was well suited to the domestic interior of the day. Small tables for writing, games and dressing were so designed that they could easily be moved by ladies. Some of his tables have adjustable screens that rise from the back to give protection from the fire. His ingenuity reaches its height with the Harlequin Pembroke table with its nest of pigeon holes and drawers which rise mechanically from the interior of the table. Designs like this and like his tambour slides and bureaux with cylinder fall fronts instead of the usual writing slope, demanded great technical ability on the part of the craftsman; the combination of Sheraton's design with craftsmanship of the highest quality produced a delicacy in cabinet work not to be found in any other period of English furniture.

Although his name is inseparably linked with the finest furniture of his age, he was not himself a craftsman nor did he have a workshop, although he did receive training as a cabinet maker. Furniture was not by any means his only interest; he was a

Inlaid mahogany serpentine-fronted sideboard in the manner of Sheraton.

preacher, an ardent Baptist who wrote a number of books and pamphlets in support of his religious views. He was born in Stockton-on-Tees in 1751 and he was forty years old before his *Cabinet Makers and Upholsterer's Drawing Book* began to be published. It came out in parts between 1791 and 1794; in 1803 he published his *Cabinet Dictionary* and then an *Encyclopaedia*. His designs embody all the lightness and elegance of Hepplewhite's furniture and take them one stage further. Some of his pieces, with their characteristic narrow tapering legs, have a delicacy that is almost brittle. But there are original ideas in Sheraton's work, and these are best seen in his chairs. Compared with other chairs of the period, his have lower and squarer backs with the horizontal top rail tenoned between the upright supports. His favourite forms of decoration were inlay, crossbanding and stringing; although he also favoured painted decoration.

His style forms the transition between the Neo-Classical and the diverse symbolism of the Regency. His search for simplicity was reinforced by the fact that England was at war during much of his working life and there was a need for a certain economy in the use of materials. But it was a period when a number of conflicting influences made themselves felt in design of all kinds. The patriotic fervour that greeted Nelson's victories found expression in a rash of nautical emblems – rope cables became. models for the carved frames of mirrors and the twisted rails in the backs of chairs; and dolphins and sea-shells, anchors and cannons were to be found in all kinds of carved decoration. The interest in Classical design was fostered by new excavations in Greece and Italy; Europe was learning more about the furniture

of the antique world and new forms of Greek and Roman ornament were becoming popular. At the same time, Napoleon was
campaigning in Egypt and Egyptian motifs – including the ubiquitous sphinx – began to appear on furniture, in England as
well as on the Continent. Finally – erratic, inconsistent but always stimulating – there was the pervasive influence of George,
Prince of Wales. He knew more about architecture, painting and
design than any prince in Europe; his tastes – and his patronage
– had far-reaching effects for craftsmen of his day.

*Carlton House writing table. A table of this type is in the Royal Collection and
is thought to have been made for Prince George's bedroom at Carlton House –
hence the name, which is first mentioned in the Gillow cost books of 1796. A
similar table, however, is to be found in Sheraton's 'Drawing Book' where it is
called a 'Lady's Drawing and writing Table'.*

Sheraton's designs reflect his sensitivity both to the needs of
domestic life and to the changes in public caprice; but by the end
of his career his reputation was fading and when he died in 1806,
he left his family, according to the *Gentleman's Magazine*, 'in dis-
tressed circumstances'. The publisher Adam Black, who was in
London in the first years of the nineteenth century, knew Sheraton well and had been employed by him to write for the *Encyclo-
paedia*. In his memoirs he says that Sheraton was a man who
understood the cabinet-making business and describes his house
as 'half shop, half dwelling'. He goes on:

> he has been and perhaps is, a preacher, he is a scholar, writes
> well, draws in my opinion masterly, is an author, book seller,
> stationer and teacher. How comes it to pass that a man of such
> abilities and resources is in such a state? I believe his abilities
> and resources are his ruin in this respect, for by attempting to
> do everything, he does nothing.

Trays, teapoys and Tunbridge Ware

It was Thomas Sheraton who defined trays as 'boards with rims round them on which to place glasses, plates, and a tea equip-age'. Trays had been used in the Middle Ages where they are described in inventories as 'voyders' and were used to carry food and plates from the table; so we find in Chippendale's *Director* of 1754 'four plans or designs for Tea Trays or voiders'. Many other cabinet makers gave considerable thought to the subject, notably Ince and Mayhew; and George Hepplewhite produced a design of great charm in 1788.

The development of tea furniture had continued for genera-tions and culminated in the teapoy of the nineteenth century. Many forms of ornament and materials were used in the creation of tea furniture. The caddies alone frequently provide master-pieces of the cabinet maker's art with a profusion of rare woods together with such surprising materials as shagreen, tortoise-shell, ivory and curled paper. Teapoys were frequently decorated with parquetry. In George Smith's *Household Furniture* published in 1808 such pieces are described as 'used in drawing-rooms to prevent the company rising from their seats when taking refresh-ments'.

Butler's tray. The tray is detachable from the stand.

Examples of caddies and teapoys are also found in Tunbridge Ware. This takes its name from Tunbridge Wells where an in-dustry producing a simple inlay of different coloured woods was started in the seventeenth century. At the end of that century the diarist Celia Fiennes wrote on her visit to the town 'the shopps in Tunbridge filled with all sorts of Curious wooden Ware which this place is noted for (the delicate neate and thin ware of wood both white and Lignum-vitae wood)'. Such inlay was initially entirely geometric, but it developed into the now well-known pictorial representations of landscapes, houses etc. with running floral borders. Lengths of coloured woods, after being cut to the required size, were glued together in a mosaic-like pattern, then cut across with a fine saw and applied as a veneer. On the same principle as seaside rock today, the pattern went right through the made-up block of woods, and thus many thin slices of veneer showing the same design could be taken from one block. Tunbridge Ware became particularly popular in Victorian times.

Demands and markets

At the turn of the century the population of England had reached ten million; one million lived in the capital. Apart from London, two towns – Liverpool and Manchester – had 100,000 inhabitants and four – Bristol, Birmingham, Leeds and Sheffield – over 50,000. The manufacturing towns were often no more than overgrown squatters' villages, spreading fast around the new steam factories, iron works and mines of the Midlands, South Lancashire and the Tyne. A German visitor in the first years of the new century has left us a picture of Birmingham: flame and smoke belching from diabolical chimneys, factories larger than palaces and every window blazing through the night as men laboured to make a hundred different artefacts – and weapons for the destruction of Bonaparte. Gleaming above the lurid town, said Herr Puckler-Muskau, were the spires of ancient churches, silhouetted in the moonlight.

In spite of this hellish picture, many of the artisans lived well. At Leek the silk workers occupied airy well-furnished apartments with carpets and oil-cloths on the floors; and Cobbett, passing through Durham and Yorkshire noted the excellence of the miners' and cutlers' homes. A weaver's apprentice wrote of his master's house:

> There were a dozen good rush-bottomed chairs, the backs and rails bright with wax and rubbing; a handsome clock in a mahogany case, a good chest of drawers, a mahogany corner cupboard, besides tables, weather-glass, cornice and ornaments and pictures illustrative of Joseph and his brethren.

The Industrial Revolution was gathering momentum yet the first thing that struck every visitor to England was the beauty of the countryside; it was still a very green land, abounding in native hardwoods – great oaks, hedgerows of elm and ash, and forest trees scattered about the meadows. Cranborne Chase had still nearly ten thousand deer; Windsor Forest, Burnham Beeches and Epping almost as many. And the countryside was the best cultivated in Europe; for a century past a succession of aristocrats, hedge squires and farmers had devoted their lives to the improvement of crops and livestock. In spite of the Enclosure Acts, every shire, every parish was cultivated as soil, climate and immemorial experience had proved best, and in the grim years that lay ahead England was able to face a long blockade and feed her ever-increasing population.

Farmers and labourers alike lived well; the standard of building in the villages was so good that the much travelled Simond noted in his journal that he could not conceive where the poor lived. The interiors of wayside cottages were furnished, he said, with elm and oak settles, iron-hooped harvest bottles, shelves for cheeses, herbs and bunches of yarn, and on the walls, brass bosses and horses' face-pieces.

The middle and lower-middle classes at the turn of the century were creating a rapidly growing market for household goods of all kinds and the furniture industry at any rate was not geared for mass production. It was a situation that called for popular design as well as for exclusive models and for new methods of production to meet the new needs. But none of these was forthcoming.

The initial impact of the machine on the English furniture industry was barely perceptible. In the early years of the nineteenth century, machines to most people – and to many craftsmen – were still an unknown quantity and they were reputed to be unreliable. They were, however, being used in naval shipyards where it was realised that they would increase output as well as reduce costs by taking over some of the back-breaking work of sawing whole tree trunks into manageable planks and rough-planing timbers of batten size.

Much of the timber imported into Britain was already sawn into boards, most of it being white deal from the Norway spruce and yellow deal from America, cut from the yellow pine. The word deal is derived from Low German and was first introduced when sawn planks began to be imported from Germany; generally speaking a deal is a slice sawn from a log that is more than seven inches wide and not more than three inches thick, but in the British timber trade it was even more closely defined: a full deal had to be nine inches wide, not more than three inches thick and at least six foot long. If it was found to be shorter it was described as a 'deal end' and if under seven inches wide, it was a 'batten'. It was for the shaping of these deals that a machine-driven saw was chiefly used.

It was not until the second half of the nineteenth century that machinery began to have any important effect on the design of furniture. Then machines were adapted for the express purpose of making handwork redundant and designs began to develop that were made to suit machine manufacture; this led inevitably to the ultimate evil – the dependence of design on the inflexible and mindless limitations of the machine itself.

The first years of the century, however, still belonged to the age of individual designers and craftsmen working in the main for a rich and discriminating clientèle.

8
The Regency

The Regent

The Prince of Wales had once been the idol of his father's subjects; Prince Charming, Prince Florizel, they called him – the First Gentleman of Europe. He was a man of great vitality and charm, cultivated, affable, handsome in his florid Hanoverian way, even witty, it was said by his Court – though courtiers are easily amused; but by the time he became Regent in 1811 a great deal of the charm and most of the popularity had disappeared; he was well on the way to becoming a public embarrassment. He was not quite fifty but he was grossly fat, an ageing Adonis who dressed in fancy uniforms of his own design, sacked housemaids if he caught them looking at his immense belly and wept at the feet of the bored beauties he still diligently pursued. But this fearful old rip was the man who sponsored the building of Regent Street and Cumberland Terrace and loved the novels of Jane Austen, was the friend of Scott, the patron of Nash. He was, said the Duke of Wellington, 'the most extraordinary compound of talent, buffoonery, obstinacy and good feeling . . . that I ever saw in any character in my life'.

All his life he spent money like water on building, statuary, carpets, paintings – he was an early collector of Dutch masters – porcelain and furniture; in three years he spent £160,000 on furniture alone. He was in fact, pre-eminent as a creator of the royal collections, adding to them not only the cream of what was made in his own lifetime but retrieving much that had been dispersed at an earlier date, including objects from the great primary collection of Charles I. He presided over the rebuilding of much of central London but perhaps his most impressive achievement was Carlton House. Here, with the help of Henry Holland, James Wyatt and John Nash, he transformed a modest two-storied mansion into a palace worthy of an Eastern potentate. When foreign ambassadors visited it in 1814 they pronounced it the finest house in England – a rival to Versailles.

Brighton Pavilion

If Carlton House was the Prince's most impressive achievement, his most characteristic was certainly Brighton Pavilion. This Oriental fantasy with its onion-shaped domes – 'looking', as Sydney Smith remarked, 'as if St Paul's had gone to the sea-side and pupped' – was one of the wonders of the age. Its combination of extravagance, vulgarity and exquisite taste reflected the very personal role the Prince had played in its design and decoration.

He had first visited Brighton in 1783 and taken a liking to the place; he amused himself by bringing the little town into fashion and in 1786 he took the lease of a converted farmhouse where he often stayed when the pressures of his father's court became too irksome. Brighton House, as it was called, was eventually to become Brighton Pavilion. The first architect to work on its conversion was Henry Holland but the elevation he created bears no relation to the one that can be seen today; his was a Palladian villa which had a central rotunda and cupola set between two wings, fine bow windows and attractive wrought iron work. In the nineteenth century however, the Prince became infatuated by the taste for Chinoiserie – now fashionable for the third time, after half a century in eclipse – and commissioned designs for a new building in the Oriental style. Several eminent architects, including Humphrey Repton, submitted drawings but the final result, build between 1815 and 1822, was the work of John Nash.

The Prince loved it: it was at once the pride of his life and his finest antidote to boredom. He had the walls decorated with mandarins and fluted yellow draperies to resemble Chinese tents, the ceilings hung with canopies of tassels and bells and he filled it with Oriental objects of all kinds, including a startling wealth of bamboo. Little of this is what it seems; what appears to be bamboo used in the architectural context – in balustrades for example – proves on handling to be cast-iron, while a large proportion of the furniture was made in England in the Chinese manner and carved and painted to simulate bamboo, though the wood is in fact beech. As the workmen had had little experience of real bamboo, these pieces are sometimes excessively adorned with painted knots.

Among the designers of furniture for the Royal Pavilion were Robert Jones, George Smith and Thomas Hope, while much of it was made by Bailey and Saunders. This London firm of cabinet makers was formerly known as Tatham and Bailey and had premises in Mount Street. The Prince was very much pleased with their side tables of rosewood and satinwood supported by Chinese dragons for use in the Banqueting Room, which cost him the 'princely' sum of £430 for each one. The same firm supplied a number of japanned chairs and some of the superb carved and gilded furniture for the Music Room.

Cross-currents

The styles and fashions of the Regency were not confined to the decade which gave them their name; the influence of the Prince made itself felt long before 1811 and certainly did not disappear when he became king in 1820. But his was not the only influence at work in the early years of the century; there were a number of others including, of course, his beloved Chinoiserie. The craze for the Gothic, which had started over fifty years before as an amusing counterpoint to the main Palladian theme, was another important trend. When Horace Walpole built Strawberry Hill – which took fifty years and was not finished until the end of the century – he meant it as an elaborate whimsy, an essay in 'venerable barbarism'; in general the Augustans despised Gothic: it was uncivilised and irrational. But the next generation, nourished on Mrs Radcliffe's *Mysteries of Udolpho* and in love with the 'picturesque', found the Neo-Gothic style exactly to its taste. It was irregular, asymmetrical and above all, romantic; William Cobbett might think it fit only for retired stock-jobbers but all over the country James Wyatt and John Nash were running up castellated mansions and ornamental cottages and landowners were commissioning carefully constructed ruins to adorn their parks. Even the Prince built himself a little place in the country, which he called York Cottage, ringed with iron-work veranda-posts and draped in creeper.

Music canterbury.

In furniture too Neo-Gothic fought for supremacy with Neo-Classicism – as well as with the styles of China, France, Egypt and Greece. Regency furniture still owed much to the designs of Hepplewhite and Sheraton from which it had evolved but there were also a number of contemporary designers who played an important part in its development. One of the most notable was Thomas Hope, a man of considerable virtuosity and erudition whose taste had been formed during his travels through Europe and the Levant.

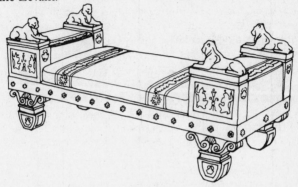

Settee by Thomas Hope, a good example of his taste and design.

Thomas Hope and George Smith

Hope was born in 1769, the son of a banker and merchant. He poured his energies and his considerable fortune into the study of architecture and into the designing and furnishing of his various houses. He carried his sketch books through Asia Minor, the Middle East and Spain and brought a scholar's perception to the adaptation of Greek and Egyptian ornament in English furniture design. He first introduced his ideas in his *Household Furniture and Interior Decoration* published in 1807. The designs were received with disapproval by contemporary critics, most of whom agreed with a writer in the *Edinburgh Review* who described the furniture as 'too bulky, massive and ponderous to be commodious for general use'. Hope found much difficulty in discovering craftsmen to carry out his ideas and finally sought the help of wood carvers and metal workers on the Continent. The furniture he designed for his house, Deepdene in Surrey, was not dispersed until July 1917, when it was sold. Since then far more general interest has been taken in the furniture and designs of Thomas Hope.

French influence is never far away from Regency furniture, and its greatest impact occurs in the early nineteenth century. Napoleon, at the height of his power, liked to identify himself with the Caesars and the splendours of the Roman Empire. French furniture of this period, which came to be known as 'French Empire', took on a new grandeur; examples and designs soon made their way to England. In the Royal Pavilion there is a superb suite of Palace furniture that demonstrates the style at its best; it is known as the Fesch suite and it once belonged to Cardinal Fesch, Napoleon's uncle, who had the family habit of 'collecting' paintings, statues and furniture wherever the Emperor's conquests made it possible.

Thomas Hope became an enthusiast for the styles of the French Empire which he found quite compatible with his taste for the antique; he had in any case strong links with France through his friendship with Charles Percier, one of the architects employed by Napoleon on the great monuments he was building in Paris; and this association did much to inspire Hope with a sense of mission to revolutionise English art forms. It was a mission that achieved some success and his *Household Furniture and Interior Decoration* helped to stimulate the interest in Classical and ancient ornament, in spite of its poor reception from the critics.

The various influences at work during the Regency affected cabinet makers in different ways. Henry Holland's furniture owes much to Adam but his free use of cast brass and ormolu mounts demonstrates his interest in the styles of the French Empire. George Smith, on the other hand, was an enthusiast for the Egyptian style.

Smith published his *Collection of Designs for Household Furniture and Interior Decoration* in 1808; four years later he published a further volume, *Collection of Ornamental Design After the Manner of the Antique*, a collection which, he considered, would be of use to 'Every Trade dependant on the Fine Arts'. For his material he drew freely on French and Classical sources as well as the work of Sheraton and Hope, but he was particularly attracted to the work of Baron Denon who had led the archaeologists accompanying Napoleon's staff during their campaign in Egypt. He was delighted by Egyptian ornament. He found it a novelty and stated that it 'gave new life to a taste for this style of embellishment'.

George Smith was a cabinet maker of considerable insight. He was a good business man and publicist and produced a further

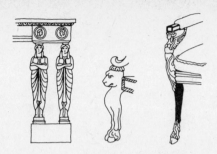

Examples of caryatid, Etruscan and Egyptian style supports.

major volume in 1828 which he called *The Cabinet Makers and Upholsterers Guide.* It was in this important volume that he noted how his earliest designs for household furniture had now been made 'wholly obsolete and inapplicable to its intended purpose, by a change of taste and rapid improvements which a period of twenty years has introduced'. It is perhaps this comment that marks Smith as one of the first men to become acutely aware of the restless shifting in design that from then on was to affect English furniture.

George Smith's pleasure in Egyptian decoration, his some-what excessive use of such motifs as the sphinx, the griffin, the lion and the leopard and his taste for palm leaves placed next to acanthus leaves all helped to give variety to his furniture and to stamp it unmistakably as a product of the Regency. The style can be seen to its best advantage in the State Dining Room at Good-wood House. This beautiful room takes its character from the pattern of its curves, which mirror one side of the room in the other, and in the delightful apse that contains the entrance door. It was here in 1814 that the Czar of all the Russias dined, together with his sister, when they came to England after Napoleon's de-feat and exile to Elba. The original decoration of this room was in the Egyptian manner, inspired by Denon whose drawings had been published in *Un Voyage dans la Basse et la Haute Egypte* in 1802. The wine coolers in this room are of sarcophagus shape, while the serving tables are in the manner of Thomas Hope and are supported by griffins. But Regency furniture, for all its ele-gance, was not always comfortable. The set of dining chairs, also original to the room, now lack the bronze crocodiles that once adorned their backs. These bronzes – still carefully retained in the Goodwood collection – were removed from the chairs at the request of Edward VII: he used the chairs whenever he visited the house during the Goodwood race meeting in July and eventually could bear their discomfort no longer.

The designers of the late eighteenth century had interpreted their classical models with some freedom; those of the Regency period copied them much more closely; and the furniture of Thomas Hope and George Smith, while it holds great fascination for the antiquarian, conveys the impression that it has stepped aside from the main tradition and development of English furniture.

One of George Smith's superb set of armchairs in the King's Apartments in the Royal Pavilion, Brighton.

Thomas Hope designed some Greek chairs which created great academic interest. Their curved legs swept away to the side and their broad semi-circular back-rests were decorated with figures copied from early vase paintings, from which the chairs themselves derived. These were not a popular success; but Classical stools did catch the public fancy. The stool itself has never gone out of favour and these, made in black and gold with lotus leaf decoration and lion paw feet, were both elegant and fashionable. In some of them portrait busts are used to form supports and pediments and though these represent contemporary personalities rather than Greek and Roman deities, the overall effect is strongly Classical.

Trafalgar and Waterloo

Nelson's victories at sea had already had their effect on English furniture and had been celebrated by Sheraton with a number of designs in his *Cabinet Dictionary* of 1803. The battle of Trafalgar in 1805 made an even greater impact. 'Trafalgar' chairs are still fashionable as dining chairs today. The back rail is often cable

Cane seat Regency chair with cable-twist rail and supports on sabre shaped legs.

moulded and the design is based on a series of sweeping curves, the back supports continuing in a curve through to the floor and the scimitar or sabre front legs curving from the front seat rails. They get their name not only from the fact that they were developed at the time of Trafalgar but also because the firm of Morgan and Saunders, one of the best cabinet-making firms of the period, renamed their premises in honour of the hero, calling them the Trafalgar Workshops.

Sarcophagus-shaped tea caddy.

Nelson's death was commemorated by innumerable mourning emblems in jewellery and porcelain; the sarcophagus tea caddies that appeared in great numbers at that date may possibly stem from Italian archaeology but the back splats of chairs shaped and carved to simulate the drapery of a sarcophagus were certainly in compliment to Nelson and it is often claimed that the lines of black stringing in the furniture of the period were also intended to do him honour.

The fashion for nautical emblems continued for more than a decade and inspired one of the most splendid suites of furniture the Regency ever produced. It was made by William Collins in 1813 and it stands in the South Drawing Room of the Royal Pavilion. It is known as the Dolphin Furniture and is splendidly carved with dolphins and other marine motifs. It was presented to the Admiralty, perhaps appropriately, by a Mrs Fish.

After the Battle of Waterloo in 1815 the Duke of Wellington became the hero of all England – a position he held in public esteem until his death nearly forty years later. The Prince Regent used the occasion to try and revive his own waning popularity and did his best to take what credit he could for Wellington's victory; as he grew older he managed to convince himself that he had actually fought at Waterloo but in 1815 he contented himself with a round of ceremonial visits and one remarkable piece of furniture the occasion produced is the State Armchair made for his visit to Walmer Castle in Kent. This magnificent object has carved front supports of winged sphinxes painted to simulate bronze.

The nation was anxious to present the Duke with an estate; he declined Uppark at Harting in Sussex, which has been called the prettiest country house in England, because of the steepness of the hill on which it stands and eventually settled on Stratfield Saye in Hampshire, which is still the home of the Dukes of Wellington. There are several fine examples of English furniture there but ironically enough the best furniture in the house is the superb collection of French pieces which the Duke took some trouble to acquire. He was particularly interested in his domestic comforts and in addition to introducing central heating and silent flush water closets to the property, he also designed the suite of reading chairs for his library.

Other Regency developments

The fashionable sofa of the Regency period was the Grecian couch, with roll curved ends, bolster cushions and carved feet. Sofa tables, which had first appeared in the late eighteenth century, now became even more popular. Unlike the Pembroke table, which has flaps on its long sides, the sofa table has flaps at the ends. Usually it has two drawers on one side and – as it was meant for use by a sofa and therefore away from the wall – two dummy drawer-fronts on the opposite side as well. The supports vary in design but perhaps the lyre-shaped ends are the most successful.

In chairs of the Regency period the broad splat back became almost universal; when the extensions of this back splat reach beyond the upright supports of the chair, it indicates a date later than 1820.

Regency writing and games table, c. 1810.

Mirrors also adopted new forms. The broad overmantels of the period often contained a large central glass flanked by two upright glasses and were sometimes surmounted by a deep gilt frieze in stucco decorated with classical figures. Pier glasses were also made with frieze panels. Another innovation of the Regency was the circular convex wall mirror; it usually had a gilded frame, often surmounted by an eagle with spread wings sometimes holding a chain in its beak from which a ball was suspended. The frames themselves were usually comparatively plain, although they were sometimes decorated with applied gilt balls around the inside edge. There are examples of these mirrors, however, which are far more ornate, enriched with acanthus leaves and

Convex wall mirror surmounted by an eagle.

even fitted with candleholders in the manner of the girandole. Hung in the dining-room, these mirrors had a practical advantage – the butler could see at a glance how the various courses were progressing.

The dining-room of the period might also contain console tables, serving tables, plant stands and cellarets but the principal piece of furniture was of course the dining table itself. At this time the most popular dining tables had rounded or D-shaped ends and were designed to allow for the insertion of extra leaves. The supports were normally in the form of a pedestal or pillar which in turn stood on tripod legs. Before about 1800 these legs had a concave line; after this date they lose their elegant sweep and rise from the pillar before curving down to brass castors; and before long the legs were replaced by plinth supports. In breakfast rooms the smaller oval and circular tables continued to be fashionable and so, in drawing rooms, did the large circular tables, sometimes heavily decorated, which were used for the game of Loo.

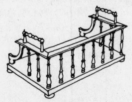

Regency rosewood book carrier, by Charles Essex, 1825.

The cabinet makers of the period preferred rich dark timbers with boldly striped figuring that would be set off to advantage by brass inlay and brass galleries, lion paw feet, lion mask handles and star-shaped bolt heads. With their generation the Classical vogue came to an end and the period that followed was one of transition, in which some designers tried to preserve the styles of the Regency while others looked ahead, affected already by the influences of the new age.

9
Victorian Mainstream

Middle-class morality

The England of the Regency, with its casual manners and still more casual morality, its passion for sport, its outspokenness and its irreverent and sardonic taste in jokes, had much in common with our own times. It is less easy to feel an affinity with the age that followed, which was dominated by a stifling respectability. Years before Victoria became queen, English society was becoming Victorian; reaction, political unrest, the Evangelical Revival – all played their part in the change; but a major cause was the growing importance of the middle class, the class that James Mill – who belonged to it – described as 'the most wise and the most virtuous part of the community'. It was this part of the community that founded the Sunday Schools, read Thomas Bowdler's *Family Shakespeare* – in which the word 'body' is replaced by the word 'person' throughout – and established the cult of a smug and orderly domesticity. In 1832 the Reform Bill was passed, setting the middle classes on the road to political power; from now on their standards and values were to be a major influence in English life.

The influence of middle-class taste on design and decoration was not always a happy one. 'Upward mobility' in the jargon of the sociologists, 'tends to result in social unease'; and social unease leads to snobbery, vulgarity and a need for display. Some of the furniture of the time appears to have been made for a clientèle which valued decoration for its quantity rather than its quality. On the other hand low standards of craftsmanship came to be accepted as furniture makers tried to keep pace with the demands of a mass market. Chairs, for example, had their straight front legs cheaply ornamented on the turning lathe, while the splayed back legs, which would otherwise have needed the time and expense of a hand carver, were left plain. By the middle of the century furniture making had grown into an industry employing thousands of workmen; virtually only Gillows continued to produce furniture on the lines of earlier days.

Cottage, farm and villa

In 1833 there appeared the first edition of J. C. Loudon's *Encyclo-paedia* of *Cottage, Farm and Villa Architecture*. It ran through ten editions in the next thirty years and had an important effect on design in the nineteenth century. Loudon was a believer in the principle of harmony between a house and its contents; he also deplored the vulgarity of taste and the shoddy workmanship of so much of the furniture of his day. His advice to his readers includes the most minute directions on the furnishing of their rooms, even down to the prints on their walls and the improving works on the shelves of the bureau bookcase, which, he said, should have its place in every cottage and villa. No detail is too small for his attention; he recommends that turned wooden knobs should be used on furniture instead of brass handles – they blend more pleasantly with the cabinet work and besides they do not tarnish.

His notes and drawings give a vivid picture – though perhaps rather an idealised one – of the smaller houses of his time and the following extracts throw interesting sidelights on existing social conditions.

614. Dressers are fixtures essential to every kitchen, but more especially to that of the cottager, to whom they serve both as dressers and sideboards. They are generally made of deal by joiners, and seldom painted, it being the pride of good house-wives, in most parts of England, to keep the boards of which they are composed as white as snow, by frequently scouring them with fine sand. The dishes, plates, etc., which they contain are also kept perfectly clean and free from dust, by being wiped every day, whether used or not. In old farmhouses, the dressers are generally of oak rubbed bright, and the shelves are filled with rows of pewter plates, etc., polished by frequent cleaning, till they shine like silver. The dresser may be called the cottager's sideboard, and in the dining rooms of the first nobleman's houses in Britain, the splendid mahogany side-boards, set out with gold and silver plate, differ only in the costliness of the materials employed from the cottage dresser; for, in Britain and America at least, good meat, good bread, and good potatoes are the main dishes on all tables, and may be obtained by the workman who has good wages and full employment, as well as by the wealthy merchant or hereditary

aristocrat. When there is a pot-board affixed to the dresser, it is usually painted black or chocolate colour; and when the shelves and fronts are painted, it is generally white, or what is in better taste, the same colours as the walls or doors of the apartment. Gothic dressers would be more appropriate if made of oak, or painted to resemble that wood. The price of a deal dresser, in London, is from £2 to £5.

620. The Furniture and Furnishing of Cottages have been hitherto neglected in every country where the comfort of the cottager has depended on those above him, and this can never be fully remedied till the inmate of the cottage is sufficiently enlightened to be able to take care of himself. We have shown, in our Chapter on Model Cottages, p. 8, that all that is essential, in point of the general arrangement of a house, may be obtained in a cottage with mud walls, as well as in palace built of marble; and we intend now to point out in what manner all that is comfortable, convenient, agreeable, and much of even what is elegant, in modern furniture and furnishing, may be formed of the indigenous woods and other common articles of every country, as well as of the most beautiful exotic timbers, and other costly materials obtained from abroad. If it should be asked, whether we expect that such Designs as those which follow can be executed or procured by the cottagers of this country, we answer that we trust they soon will be; and we believe that the first step towards this desirable end is, to teach them what to wish for. As the spread of knowledge becomes general, it will be accompanied by the spread of taste; and correct habits of thinking will go hand in hand with comfortable dwellings, and convenient, neat and elegant forms of furniture. An approximation to equalisation in knowledge will lead to an approximation in every thing else; for knowledge is power, and the first use which every man makes of it is, to endeavour to better his own condition. Our grand object, therefore, in this as in every other department of our work, is to cooperate with the causes at present in operation for bettering the condition, and elevating the character, of the great mass of society in all countries. Though most of the Designs submitted are of a superior description to what are common in cottages, they are not on that account more expensive than various cumbrous articles of furniture now possessed or desired by every cottager in tolerable circumstances. The difference will be found to consist chiefly in the kind of labour employed in making them, and in the style of design which they exhibit.

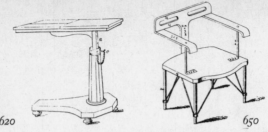

620   650

Fig. 620, to a scale of half an inch to a foot, is a table for invalids, commonly called a bed table; which is a very great convenience to a person bedridden. The top of this table is made to rise and fall at pleasure, by raising or lowering the upper part of the pillar, a, which is perforated with holes at given distances, and which works in a square groove, in the centre of the lower part. This lower part is formed of four pieces glued together, as shown in the plan, b, in fig. 621. It is firmly fixed in the bottom block of a mortise and tenon, and at the top the four pieces are confined by an iron ferrule, to keep the joints from opening; the mortise at bottom sufficiently confines the lower part of the pillar. The height of the top is regulated by moving the pin at c: the block or foot, of which d represents a plan, is elongated on one side to about the same extent as the top is elongated on that side; and, when the table is in use, the block is turned under the bed, and the top over it; the latter being adjusted to the height most convenient for the patient. This table is very frequently used for reading in bed; and in that case it is generally made with a horse and rack, e, and a shifting ledge, f, to support a book, at one end. This ledge is fixed by two wire pins, fastened in its under side, which drop into two holes bored in the lower side of the flap of the table. On the edge of this ledge are affixed two book-holders, g, commonly made of brass, but which are much better if made of ivory, or of ebony, box, or any other hard wood. This table, in mahogany, costs in London from £5 to £7; but, made of any common wood by a joiner in the country, it would not come to half the amount.

Fig. 650 is a Design for an iron elbow kitchen chair, by Mr. Mallet. The back and elbows are cast in one piece; the supports for the elbows and also the legs are of gas tubing, screwed into a cross frame of iron, which proceeds from the back of the chair under the wooden seat. This is a strong, durable, and cheap chair, and only wants good cushions, for the back, elbows, and seat, to render it a most comfortable article for a cottager.

683. Geographical Carpets. The idea of a geographical carpet, that is, a carpet with the lines of a map substituted for a regular pattern, have been suggested (Mech. Mag., col. xii p. 21); and we agree with the author of the suggestion in thinking that 'a carpet is so admirably adapted to geographical instruction, that it may be almost said to be a natural article for the purpose. A map is a picture of the surface of the earth, and on the ground is the place to view it. One on so large a scale as a carpet would admit, is calculated to give a more correct idea of the relative position of places than could be effected by the largest map now extant. A family in the daily occupation of a room furnished with such a carpet, would acquire unavoidably a more permanent knowledge of a given portion of the earth than could be obtained by any other means; and, when the local position of the room would admit, the carpet might be placed agreeably to the bearings of the compass, and it would thereby give a correct idea of the real direction of places on the map'.

1250

1376. The Introduction of Iron into the Furniture of Farmhouses would be attended with considerable economy, at least in the article of dining tables, sideboards, bedsteads and hall, lobby, or porch chairs. The sideboards may be formed of slabs of native marble in some districts, and slate in others, supported by enriched cast-iron feet, *fig. 1249*, or by brackets of various kinds, *fig. 1250*. Sideboards of this kind have a massive architectural effect, very suitable for all houses whatever, and especially for houses in the country, where room is not an object. For our own part, we should even prefer slabs of finely polished stone, as sideboards, to wood of any kind; but cast-iron may be substituted; and, where neither metal nor stone is approved of, wood of some kind is always to be obtained, and may be worked and polished at pleasure.

1251

Fig. 1251 is a circular table, the top of which may be made of mahogany, or any other finely grained wood, and the supports of cast-iron bronzed. The idea of having iron bedsteads will, we have no doubt, shock those who have been always accustomed to consider mahogany as essential for this piece of furniture: but we can assure them that they are to be found in the houses of people of wealth and fashion in London; sometimes even for the best beds.

1942

2113. Chiffoniers. *Fig. 1942* is a chiffonier pier table for placing between windows. These tables are usually finished with white marble tops, with plate glass behind, and a shelf supported by brackets for holding ornaments. The panels of the doors may be silvered plate glass, or of fluted silk. These are most useful objects for families who cannot afford to go to the expense of pier or console tables. In parlours, and even lady's libraries, they may be used as a sort of morning sideboard for containing any light species of refreshment.

1945

2114. Davenports (so called from the inventor's name) are drawing room writing cabinets used by ladies. *Fig. 1945* is a very convenient piece of furniture of this description, the top part, forming the desk, pulls forward to come over the knees when it is to be used. A sliding flap draws out on each side, to hold papers, a candle, etc. The desk lid lifts up, and beneath it is a space for papers, and several small drawers. There is besides a drawer which pulls out at the side, and turns round, as shown in the figure, for pens, inks, wafers, etc. Beneath the flap are drawers on one side, and the other side is finished with the appearance of drawers to correspond. The back is handsomely panelled, so that each side of this piece of furniture looks well. The flaps and sides are lined with morocco leather embossed. There are castors concealed in the feet.

1946

Fig. 1946 is a Davenport which stands on a plinth, having concealed castors, and which resembles the preceding one in every respect, except in being rather plainer. These are very useful articles for industrious young ladies.

1999

2145. Chairs are the next articles made use of by children; and those about London are of four kinds. *Fig. 1999* is a child's chair of the first kind, having a night pan, and a matted seat. A small stuffed flannel of the size of the seat, and having a round hole in the centre, is generally placed over it when it is to be used, in order to prevent the pan from hurting the child. (In some districts of Italy, and other parts of the Continent, rings of stuffed cloth, or stuffed leather, or of rush matting, are used for the same purpose by grown-up persons.) In England, infants of ordinary health and strength are put into chairs of this kind, when between three and four months old.

2000

Fig. 2000 is an Astley Cooper's chair being a form recommended by that eminent surgeon, with the view of preventing children from acquiring a habit of leaning forward, or stooping; the upright position of the back affording support when the child is placed at table, and eating, which a sloping-backed chair does not. It is proper to observe that some medical men do not approve of these chairs.

2001

Fig. 2001 is a child's elbow-chair, or bergère, as it is commonly called in England. This chair stands on a stool, to which it is attached by a thumb-screw; and, when the chair is removed from the stool, the latter forms a table for the child to put its playthings on. The shelf for the feet is made to move higher or lower as may be required. The chair is only fixed on the stool when the child is to sit at table to eat, which it may do when about eighteen months of age.

Rose-tinted spectacles

The cottage Homes of England . . .
Through glowing orchards forth they peep,
Each from its nook of leaves,
And fearless there the lowly sleep,
As the bird beneath their eaves . . .

   Mrs Hemans.

The rosy picture painted by Mrs Hemans of the cottage homes of England had little to do with reality; rural prosperity had collapsed after the French wars and the housing of farm labourers became a national scandal. Many of them were forced to live in their masters' houses and were unable to marry until late in life, if they married at all. But even this was better than being homeless. In 1833 Cobbett found that many of them were being driven into insanitary hovels by the 'shoal of ostentatious fooleries' of the farmers' wives. As the economy recovered and the farmer's income increased, so did his wife's pretensions. In a farmhouse where there had once been plain manners, Cobbett wrote, 'there was now a parlour and mahogany tables. Aye, and a carpet and a bell-pull too'. The newly genteel lady of the house naturally could not tolerate labourers tramping about on her new carpets; so, says Cobbett, she turned them out to find what shelter they might.

   Loudon's paternalistic intention to 'teach Cottagers what they should wish for' must have seemed a little ironic when it was first published. It was not until the mid century that farm labourers' housing began to improve and model cottages were built on any great scale; in the meantime the farm labourer usually lived in rural squalor – which was still preferable, however, to the squalor of the London slums, where it was not unusual for a family of ten to live in one room.

Victorian Gothic

By the time the Prince Regent became king, Neo-Gothic – like so much else – had begun to acquire a high moral purpose. In 1818 an act was passed by which the state allocated a million pounds to the building of new churches as strongholds against dissent and democracy. Two hundred and fourteen were built, a hundred and seventy-four of them in the Gothic style, mostly in brick and many with cast iron columns supporting the galleries. Gothic was cheap; the *Gentleman's Magazine* of that year told its readers that: 'there is scarcely an ornament or a necessary part

Mahogany breakfront bookcase with Gothic style ornament, c. 1830.

but what might be cast at one Iron Foundry; even the highest wrought filigree Gothic'. In 1819 the bastard style was legitimised and given a new name. Thomas Rickman's *Attempt to Discriminate the Styles of English Architecture* called it Early English which perhaps lends colour to the theory that an effort was being made to find an English national style. Whatever its name, it continued to be popular. Walter Scott's novels fostered the enthusiasm for medieval and Elizabethan romance and now Elizabethan styles became fashionable too. His own house, Abbotsford, had a number of Elizabethan features, which assorted rather oddly with Scottish Baronial.

In 1835 a recommendation was made that the Palace of Westminster should be rebuilt in the Gothic and Elizabethan styles and Augustus Welby Pugin helped to design the new Houses of Parliament between 1837 and 1843. Colleges, railway stations and town halls rose up all over England adorned with pointed arches, perforated iron work and roof lines pricked into crockets and pinnacles; but the Gothic mania found its principal outlet in churches. The Rector of Buckland in Devon went so far as to pull down the genuine medieval church in his parish and replace it with a new, very ornate, very Gothic structure which was consecrated in 1863. The Puseyite movement, spreading from Oxford, with its revival of Catholic ritual, its painted chancels, niches, candles and stained glass windows, naturally preferred Gothic to the sober Hanoverian churches with no Catholic associations; and although ecclesiastical Gothic looks what it is – mock – it remained the principal motive power of the Victorian builders.

Architects in the nineteenth century were still among the leaders of furniture design; in the thirties A. C. Pugin published *Gothic Furniture*; his drawings, as might be expected, were lavishly adorned with pinnacles, crockets, tracery and gables, which he applied freely and without discrimination to all kinds of furniture. In 1836 Henry Shaw published his *Specimens of Ancient Furniture*; it consisted mainly of English examples that ranged from Gothic to Restoration. Both these works helped to perpetuate the vogue for pastiche which, combined with the Victorian taste for display, did so much to vulgarise nineteenth-century furniture.

The Great Exhibition

In the eighteenth century Josiah Wedgwood had seen that good design and workmanship were bound to come into conflict with the demands of mass-production but it was his dictum that: 'because an object is useful, that is no reason for it to be ugly'; and he employed artists to design his pottery. In the 1830's other manufacturers began to share his concern and good design soon became a matter of public interest. In 1837 the School of Design was opened at Somerset House and similar establishments soon followed in the provinces. New magazines began to appear: *The Builder* in 1843, *Art Union* from 1844 to 1848, the *Art Journal* in 1849 and the *Journal of Design Manufactures* from 1849 to 1852. They acted as critics both of education in design and of design itself; they published new designs and provided a shop window for the exhibitions set up by manufacturers. The way was being prepared for the Great Exhibition.

In 1843 a Royal Commission was set up to enquire into ways of encouraging the arts of the United Kingdom and Sir Robert Peel invited Prince Albert to preside over it. It was an inspired choice. In his life of Queen Victoria, Lytton Strachey comments:

> The work was of a kind which precisely suited Albert: his love of art, his love of method, his love of coming into contact – close yet dignified – with distinguished men – it satisfied them all; and he threw himself into it 'con amore'. When the question arose as to whether the decorations of the new buildings should, or should not have a moral purpose, the Prince spoke strongly in the affirmative.

But his views and his influence went a great deal further than that. Housing, furniture, domestic economy were all among the Prince's interests; he had re-organised the Queen's household affairs so successfully that when they wanted a retreat from the pomp of Windsor – somewhere remote and intimate – they were able to buy the estate of Osborne on the Isle of Wight, build themselves a house there and furnish it at a cost of £200,000 – all out of their savings. And the Prince, in collaboration with the builder Thomas Cubitt, had designed the house.

The public, says Lytton Strachey, looked on with approval. At the time of his marriage, the Prince had not been popular; now his uplifting influence was plain to everyone. The Queen no longer enjoyed late hours and London parties; every spare hour was spent at Osborne, by the sea and among the woods that Albert had so carefully planted. Strachey comments:

> A few aristocrats might sniff and titter but the middle-classes. ... liked a household which combined the advantages of royalty and virtue and in which they seemed to see the ideal image of the very lives they led themselves. Their own exist-ence acquired an added excellence ... from the early hours, the regularity, the plain tuckers, the round games, the roast beef and Yorkshire pudding of Osborne.

Duty, industry, morality and domesticity had triumphed.

> Even the very chairs and tables, with singular responsiveness, had assumed the forms of prim solidity. The Victorian Age was in full swing ...
>
> Only one thing more was needed: material expression must be given to the new ideals and the new forces ... It was for Albert to supply the want. He mused and was inspired: the Great Exhibition came into his head.

It was to show the world what every country could produce in raw materials and machinery, in manufacture and the applied and plastic arts; above all it was to provide a market place where the buyers of the world could see the very best in British design. The Prince summoned a small committee and laid his scheme before it; the great undertaking was set in motion without delay.

Out of 234 plans for the Exhibition building, the Prince chose that of Joseph Paxton who submitted a design for a gigantic con-servatory – nearly a million square feet of glass fastened on to thirty miles of iron frame which eventually encompassed within its span several mature elm trees as well as the 15,000 exhibits. It owed its existence to a botanical prodigy. The huge water lily, Victoria Regia, was discovered in British Guiana in 1836 and in 1849 plants were successfully grown at Kew. An example sent to the Duke of Devonshire at Chatsworth flowered the same year, the first to do so in England. The speed with which the giant lily grew made it essential for a new conservatory to be built to house it, and it was the simple modular design of this building that Joseph Paxton, the head gardener at Chatsworth, was to expand later into the Crystal Palace.

Paxton (1803–1865) was one of the most extraordinary men of the nineteenth century. The son of a Bedfordshire farmer, he became head gardener at Chatsworth in 1826 and he also acted as agent, engineer and architect. It was Paxton who designed Mentmore, in Buckinghamshire, from which a superb collection of furniture belonging to the Rothschild family was sold in 1977. He was knighted in 1851, was associated with the development of the Midland railway and elected Member of Parliament for Coventry in 1854. He was not, it appears, a man to let the grass grow under his feet. When he first arrived at Chatsworth in the early hours of the morning on 9 May 1826, he climbed the estate wall and, after exploring the garden, set the gardeners to work at six o'clock; he retired to the house for breakfast with the house-keeper and her niece, Sarah Brown. According to Paxton's own account:

> The Latter fell in love with me and I with her, and thus completed my first morning's work at Chatsworth before 9 o'clock.

The Prince and his coadjutor, Henry Cole of the Society of Arts, did not find their task an easy one. There was an outcry, led by *The Times*, against the use of Hyde Park, the chosen site for the Exhibition. After a fierce debate in the House, the supporters of the Park won the day. Then it seemed there would be insufficient funds; eventually £200,000 was subscribed. There was an outcry from the numerous opponents of the project – all the ruffians in Europe would use the Exhibition as a rallying point, they said; there would be an outbreak of plague, a riot – probably a revolution; the Crystal Palace would be struck by lightning; the glass was porous and the droppings of fifty million sparrows would inevitably destroy every object beneath it. The Queen herself mentioned this last objection to the Duke of Wellington, who replied briskly: 'Try sparrowhawks, Ma'am.' The Prince and his committee laboured on and eventually, on 1 May 1851, the Great Exhibition was opened by the Queen amid scenes of triumphant enthusiasm.

The exhibits were arranged in four classes: sculpture and fine arts; machinery; manufactures and raw materials. Six million people came to see them; even the scoffers were converted and Queen Victoria wrote in her diary:

> The first of May was the *greatest* day in our history . . . the *happiest* and *proudest* day of my life. Albert's dearest name is immortalised with this *great* conception, *his* own. . . . The triumph is *immense.*

Among the exhibits were some 'Model Cottages' designed by the Prince himself, which were re-erected after the Exhibition in Kennington Park. There was also, of course, a wide variety of furniture; but the English furniture makers had completely misunderstood the part they were supposed to play in the enterprise. They produced grand exhibition pieces of great size and elaborate design rather than simple objects for everyday use; nevertheless the Exhibition provided a great stimulus to new techniques of construction which made dramatic changes in the development of nineteenth-century furniture.

The Crystal Palace at the time of the Great Exhibition in Hyde Park, 1851.

The main types of woodworking machines had already been invented by the beginning of Queen Victoria's reign, but it was not until after the Great Exhibition that they were widely used. Certain of these machines led to an immediate fall in quality. The veneer-cutting machine meant that veneer could easily be used to cover up poor construction. Wood-carving machines also deprived many hand carvers of their work and removed the influence of the individual craftsman from a great deal of furniture. More substitutes were discovered for expensive materials, such as cheap imitations of ormolu and timbers such as beech stained to simulate rosewood. Yet in spite of the proliferation of poorer quality products there is much Victorian furniture of outstanding quality; moreover without the machines Victorians of all classes would never have been able to furnish their houses with the variety and comfort they did.

Papier-mâché

The nineteenth century was a highly experimental period, particularly in the investigation of new materials that might be of use to the cabinet maker. Many of them were unsuccessful but some interesting and worthwhile results were obtained from the use of papier-mâché. Papier-mâché had been used long before in the East and was introduced into England from France. It consisted then of a paper pulp mixed with chalk, glue and occasionally fine sand; when pressed and baked it achieved such a degree of hardness that it could be sawn and polished. The French, for example, made snuff boxes of it in the eighteenth century and it was also used for picture frames; but it was Henry Clay of Birmingham who, in 1772, perfected a form of papier-mâché which was strong enough to be used in furniture construction. Very often Clay's invention was not referred to as papier-mâché at all, but as 'Clay's-ware'. Clay is believed to have left Birmingham in 1802 and opened a shop in London for the sale of furniture made by his process. In the accounts of Osterley Park there is an entry for four guineas paid in 1804 to 'Henry Clay, japanner in ordinary to His Majesty'.

Papier-mâché chair.

The framework of a chair would be made in iron covered with paper pulp and then, after being dressed with pitch and oil, brought to a high temperature and allowed to cool. This process was repeated until the required thickness of paper was obtained. It could then be japanned and inlaid with mother-of-pearl and very fine decorative effects obtained. It proved to be a material of great strength and was popular for occasional chairs and tables. Entire bedroom suites were even constructed of this material.

Henry Clay was careful to note the difference between his own work and the original papier-mâché. Clay named his own product 'paper ware', but in the 1830's the firm of Jennens and Bettridge decided that the French name (meaning pulped paper) was a better description – if not entirely accurate. Jennens and Bettridge were major producers of this ware which was at the height of its popularity between 1835 and 1870. There is a certain likeness between the papier-mâché work of this period and the japanned productions of the seventeenth century.

In a section given to the papier-mâché trade by the Pearson and Rollason *Directory* for 1781, a reference to Henry Clay's manufacturing states that:

> several pieces of superb furniture, which now adorn the royal residence had been made and that King George III seemed happy in expressing his utmost approbation ... and His Majesty, with a condescension and liberality becoming the patron of the polite and useful arts, has been pleased to grant him letters of patent, thereby giving him the sole and exclusive privilege of manufacturing in paper, certain articles in which the dovetail joint is used.

Clay declared that his new improved paperware would be 'sawn, planed, dovetailed or mitred in the same manner as if made in wood'. His work is marked with 'Clay Patent' impressed with a crown, or 'Clay, King Street, Covent Garden'.

The firm W. Clay & Sons of Fenchurch Street, who were descendants of Henry Clay, had their showrooms in the Haymarket and exhibited papier-mâché furniture at the Great Exhibition. A mass of such furniture was displayed at the Great Exhibition including sofas, chairs, a variety of tables, stools, Canterburys, cabinets, beds, cradles, chiffoniers, pole-screens, cases for grand pianos and cheval mirrors. Some items were composed entirely of papier-mâché, but Joseph Bettridge had introduced a method in 1841 of applying a substantial layer of papier-mâché over a stove-dried wood frame and this form of construction was also on show. It was used particularly for tables as it was far more swift and convenient than baking the table-top, support and base on iron moulds and then joining them together.

Chairs made in this way follow traditional lines, the best of them having the entire back moulded from papier-mâché but the legs reinforced with a wooden core; the finished work was lightly gilded or painted with sprays of flowers and possibly inlaid with mother-of-pearl. The cane-seated chairs, having wooden frames lightly overlaid with papier-mâché, were very cheap examples of the art and appear to have been made between 1870 and 1880. Some excellent pictorial scenes may be found painted on flat surfaces of papier-mâché furniture, but it should be remembered that in 1842 George Goodman of Birmingham developed a process for transferring painted copies of pictures from engraved plates on to paper which were then fastened on to the papier-mâché and given coats of varnish to seal them. Papier-mâché furniture will frequently bear a registration number and the finer examples, the impressed mark 'Jennens and Bettridge, London'.

Old styles and new designs

The Great Exhibition had given its six million visitors the opportunity to see fashions from abroad as well as all that was newest in English furniture design and construction. The coming of the railways made travel possible to more people than ever before; it widened their horizons and encouraged their interest in new ideas. The result of all this was a great diversity in the design of Victorian furniture, although much of it took the form of new variations on well-established themes. A. W. Pugin's designs in

Carved oak dining chair upholstered in imitation leather.
Designed by A. W. Pugin.

the Gothic style were well suited to the ecclesiastical tone of the day and his stools, chairs, cabinets and tables are outstanding among early Victorian pieces; they also exemplify a kind of restrained carving that does not conceal the structure of the furniture itself – as well as a comprehensive knowledge of sixteenth-century design soundly used to suit contemporary needs.

The sideboard, that symbol of good living, was usually extremely solid in Victorian times and sometimes embellished with a mirror back; but the chiffonier, which had evolved during the early part of the century, appeared in a wide variety of styles. The Regency hallstand had given way to a larger version, constructed to stand against the wall; mirrors were added to it and box-top compartments and sometimes drawers and drip pans for sticks and umbrellas. It was popular, with many variations, right through the Victorian era and well into the twentieth century.

Victorian hallstand.

The remarkable differences between the various styles of nineteenth-century furniture could sometimes blend with good effect. A visit to Osborne House, on the Isle of Wight, and to the room in which Queen Victoria and Prince Albert wrote side by side at their desks, demonstrates this very well. Whatnots, unmatching tables, balloon-back and 'Elizabethan' chairs produce an acceptable and interesting confusion.

Individual designers also exhibited astonishing fluctuations in their work. Henry Eyles of Bath, who exhibited several pieces in the Great Exhibition, is a good example. He produced a low-seated, carved walnut armchair with a porcelain plaque of Prince

Whatnot.

Albert set in the back. The chair was also carved with a mass of naturalistic ornament and gives a general appearance of being both squat and heavy. The single chair in the same set, however, has carved and inlaid walnut and again the porcelain plaque featuring at the back – this time painted with a full length portrait of Queen Victoria; it also carries naturalistic carving, and the cabriole front legs and scroll feet contribute to a chair that can only be described as elegant.

The Royal family itself contributed one theme to the general confusion of design in the mid-century. Ever since her first visit to Scotland early in her marriage, the Queen had felt her heart was in the Highlands. In 1848 she took the lease of a little old house at Balmoral in the wilds of Aberdeenshire; but the Prince decided to pull it down and replace it with a castle of his own design. It was built of granite in the Scotch Baronial style, with turrets and castellated gables and a tower a hundred feet high; and it commanded splendid views over the river Dee. The Queen and the Prince took immense pains over the interior. The walls and floors were of pitch-pine and in the hall, together with innumerable stags antlers, was a life-size statue of Albert in Highland dress. For the décor Victoria herself designed a tartan, and there were tartan carpets and tartan curtains and tartan chair-covers; and in 1860, when linoleum was invented, there were tartan linoleums too.

The Highland mania soon spread South and tartans, thistles, antlers and cairngorms became the rage in England as well.

The Warwick School

Among the mass of heavily carved furniture so beloved by the Victorians, there is one outstanding group of pieces belonging to what is known as the Warwick School of carving. The art of wood-carving by hand had been revived in the 1840's – a revival almost certainly inspired by W. G. Rogers who had developed his craft during the Regency and had continued to exercise it while many of his contemporaries were going out of business. He had trained his two sons as carvers and they carried on the family skill. Prince Albert was interested in wood-carving – as became a German prince – and he and the Queen bestowed their patronage on Rogers. It may well have been his work which suggested to the Prince that a prize should be offered by the Society of Arts for amateur carvers.

There was now a strong feeling against the use of machinery as the only means of furniture construction. The town of Warwick had become established as a major source of fine furniture in the provinces and carving, particularly on larger pieces of furniture such as overmantels, sideboards, buffets and cupboards, became a speciality of the town. It became so important that, when examining the major examples of Warwick School pieces, it is difficult to draw a line between sculpture and furniture. In the 1851 Exhibition William Cookes, a carver from Warwick, became famous for his 'Kenilworth' Buffet, a great sideboard carved with scenes from Scott's novel. In the Exhibition of 1862 Thomas Tweedy, of Newcastle-on-Tyne, showed two sideboards; one illustrated Robinson Crusoe; the other, themes from Shakespeare. Thomas Tweedy's apprentice and later foreman, Gerrard Robinson, was commissioned by the Duke of Northumberland to produce a major carved piece and the result was the Chevy Chase sideboard exhibited in London in 1865. Robinson was a remarkable man who was to continue as a carver for the next twenty-five years and the Chevy Chase sideboard is probably the most celebrated example of nineteenth-century carving in Britain. These narrative carvings were extremely popular for a time but the carver needed large pieces of furniture if he was to have adequate scope for his subject; the later decline in very large furniture spelt the end of the carving tradition and it played little part in the decoration of furniture in the early twentieth century.

Sofas and settees

During the reign of William IV both the double-ended Grecian sofa and the scroll-ended variety had continued to be popular, although within a very few years such furniture was to become over stuffed, over carved, and generally debased. The outward-curving supports which had previously been such a feature of the Regency soon developed into stump-like legs mounted on heavy castors. Louis XV style sofas were made in some quantity, usual-

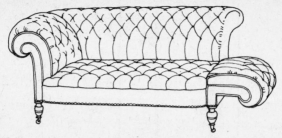

Chesterfield settee, known as the 'Ambidexter'. The ends could be adjusted to any angle for use as an impromptu bed.

ly with upholstered seats and ends, having a padded centre panel back joined by pierced and carved sections. But the French style single-end sofa with its mahogany frame, often described today as a show-wood frame, was surprisingly common. The frame, no matter what timber may be used in construction, is termed 'show-wood' simply because it has not been hidden by the upholstery. The French influence was soon eliminated from the design and at the end of the century Britain bulged with a surfeit of right-arm couches, the bulk of which were poorly covered, a large proportion in American cloth. Even in the early years of the twentieth century American cloth was widely used to upholster seat furniture, particularly that which faced hard wear in public rooms; many such chairs, sofas and couches furnished the bars of the English public house. Before the later nineteenth-century reintroduction of Georgian-style sofas, the button-upholstered Chesterfield with its drop-end ensured the comfort of the Victorian sitting room – as did the use of sprung seats.

There were also, of course, finely made and richly upholstered examples of the couch, although a more accurate name might be 'single-ended day bed'. In such a piece one would expect to find deeply buttoned upholstery and a good mahogany show-wood frame, the ends terminating in rich Baroque scrolls. The Conversation settee and the Ottoman (a form of chest which has a padded top) were often upholstered in the same manner and were both in great demand.

Tables

Occasional tables continued to be as popular as they had been in the Regency; they were used for a wide variety of purposes and made in many different designs and materials. Walnut veneer was much in demand; four-legged mahogany tea tables with

'Gipsy' table on turned supports.

undershelves frequently had turned legs to simulate bamboo, and a mass of genuine Oriental bamboo chairs and tables were also available on the market. Large mahogany dining tables on turned legs were well suited to the size of the families of the times, while in the large kitchens, and in many rooms of more humble homes, pine was frequently used. Much Victorian pine furniture was stained or painted and this, one hundred years later, was to create something almost of a cottage industry among those wishing to strip such pieces in order to reveal the colour and grain of the pine itself. Small tripod tables and eight-legged circular tables were popular; so were shaped-top circular tables on bobbin-turned tripod or 'cat' supports. There were many variations of eighteenth-century designs, together with outright copies, with cabinet work of the highest quality. Much furniture in the French style was also made in England with great accuracy. Sutherland tables were also well liked and remain most useful and distinctive pieces of furniture. They are fall-leaf tables with an exceedingly narrow top, the leaves being deep and long. Victorian Loo tables are also popular to-day, particularly when they are made of finely figured rosewood. They are now often used as dining tables and most of them have the added

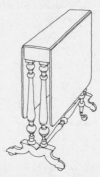

Sutherland table.

advantage that their wide diameter tops can be tilted so that the table can be pushed against the wall when it is not in use.

Chairs

It is no longer fashionable to condemn all Victorian furniture as vulgar and tasteless as so many people did in the first half of this century. Some Victorian chairs are as popular now as they were when they were first made. One example is the upholstered chair with a mahogany show-wood frame, which in fact derives from the French eighteenth-century elbow chair or fauteuil. Some of them are as large and deep as easy chairs; some are small tub chairs. Both are extremely comfortable. The decoration to the frame is usually slight; scrolls are used on the arms and the best examples are set on well-carved cabriole legs and scroll feet.

The Victorians themselves, of course, were very much interested in the furniture of the past and about 1840 the famous Indo-Portuguese chair given by Charles II to Elias Ashmole was reproduced in turned and carved ebony. It was probably copied from one of the illustrations in Henry Shaw's book *Ancient Furniture* and may well have been considered to be 'Elizabethan'.

Much of the early Victorian seat furniture was designed with the crinoline in mind and many low-seated chairs are to be seen today that would originally have been called ladies' chairs. Some of the very low-seated examples may well be nursing chairs. Another specialised type of chair which was much in vogue in households in the grip of the Oxford Movement was the prie-dieu, a chair designed for prayer, on which the user knelt. It has

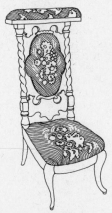

Prie-dieu chair upholstered in Berlin tapestry.

a distinctive tall narrow back and an upholstered top rail, providing an arm rest. All kinds of material were used in the construction and decoration of the prie-dieu and some of the most interesting specimens are those executed in papier-mâché or upholstered in bead work or Berlin tapestry.

Berlinwork was also used to decorate chairs made in the Stuart manner, with turned legs and supports and high turned backs. It appeared on the stuffed seats and the centre back panels; and sometimes on antimacassars as well. In the early nineteenth century a Berlin print seller had begun to issue squared patterns that could be copied on to canvas and embroidered in either cross or tent stitch. Many of the themes were of a religious nature and the work made a suitably uplifting pastime for the ladies of the household. But there was plenty of scope in the Victorian home for needlework of other kinds as well – fringes for the edges of the mantelpiece, valences for the sofa and frilly skirts to cover up the knees and legs of machine-carved piano cases.

The later Victorian easy chairs tend to be of somewhat squat proportions and are frequently totally lacking in style, although this is not true of the small horseshoe backed chairs, with circular upholstered seats, padded back rest and arms, developed during the 1870's. Upholstered single chairs that were part of Victorian drawing room furniture also possess a lasting charm; the type known as balloon-back are among the best of them, especially when executed in walnut or rosewood. Many simulated rosewood examples are to be seen and a number of such chairs were also made in mahogany; these chairs were fashionable from the beginning of Queen Victoria's reign for well over a generation. Balloon-back chairs are perhaps at their

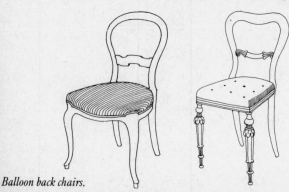

Balloon back chairs.

most successful when they have cabriole legs; these became popular from the 1850's onwards. Dining-room chairs were often made with the broad shoulder-board which in the early part of the century had extended like ears beyond the back supports (a sure sign of nineteenth-century origin). But they soon developed shaped boards with rounded ends that linked the back supports – still overlapping. Finer examples tend to be lightly carved and set on turned and fluted legs, while later examples usually have heavier vase-shaped turning or heavy reeding.

Children's furniture has a perennial charm and the Victorian child's chair is no exception. The elegant little chair designed by Sir Astley Cooper, which Loudon mentions in his book, is known today as a deportment chair. It has a high straight back and bears eloquent witness to parental fears of curvature of the spine. In the teeth of much contemporary medical opinion, some Victorian children were drilled into a correct posture by the use of these chairs, just as their elder sisters were drilled by the use of the backboard, a piece of furniture that had a place in almost every Victorian schoolroom. It consisted of a wooden board, thinly upholstered, which was supported on a framework at an angle of forty-five degrees from the floor. Halfway down was a narrow ledge, to prevent the user from sliding off. Growing girls used to recline on the board for hours on end in the interests of an elegant and upright carriage.

There were a number of other types of chair in common use, made in a diversity of styles, some of them Victorian versions of earlier designs. The Louis XV style was one of the most successful; of those in the Gothic or Elizabethan idiom, hall chairs show some design elements of particular interest.

Late Victorian trends

There were forces at work in the second half of Victoria's reign that were sapping away at the very foundations of the solid and confident England she ruled; the rise of socialism, the spread of religious doubt, the Married Women's Property Act and the invention of birth control would eventually undermine three of the pillars of Victorian society. But in the meantime, for the vast majority of middle-class England, power and money seemed still to be in the right hands; the Established Church was the arbiter of faith and morals and marriage and the family were sacrosanct.

They lived, many of these 'early Forsytes', in large houses in Kensington or Bayswater or in comfortable suburban properties with carriage sweeps and shrubberies and croquet lawns. The furniture that survives from that period makes it easy to imagine the interiors of those houses: the chiffoniers in mahogany, rosewood or walnut veneers with their shelf tops on double scroll supports; the whatnots; the flower stands and jardinières; the glazed display cabinets; the heavy breakfront mahogany bookcases and their dwarf counterparts with ornamental soft leather fringes hanging below each shelf to shield the gilded edges of the books from dust; fire screens; and desks of all kinds and sizes. There are Davenports – far removed from the clean lines of the original design by Gillow; there are mahogany bureaux and mahogany and oak knee-hole desks with pillar supports and drawers and small turned wooden handles. And from Victorian bedrooms, there are mahogany dressing tables and marble-topped bedside cupboards and wash-stands.

Just as the Victorians were guilty of 'carving up' undecorated examples of early furniture and sometimes of adapting them to new uses, so the twentieth century has been responsible for altering many Victorian pieces. Mahogany wash-stands and dressing tables have had their fittings removed and leather panels fitted so that they may be sold as 'Victorian writing tables'. Many of the exceedingly large but beautifully made Victorian wardrobes have been broken up, sometimes to be converted but more often so that the well-seasoned timber can be used either to make new furniture or to restore old pieces.

Carved and painted washstand with fittings of marble and bronze, designed by William Burges, 1880.

There are many small examples in the second half of the nineteenth century that show Victorian craftsmanship at its best: the book carrier, for instance. At the beginning of the nineteenth century superb Regency book carriers were made; these enabled a lady, perhaps, to carry her favourite volumes from room to room. Similar examples appeared later in the century, most of them in the Gothic style and exquisitely finished. So too are the storage cabinets and display cases made to contain the treasures of the Victorian collector. It was the day of the cultivated amateur with his collections of sea-shells, minerals, coins, plants, butterflies etc. It was also the age of the 'souvenir', and cabinets and shelves were needed to display such things to advantage. But while many of the smaller pieces of furniture are of a size that appeals to the twentieth-century furnisher, it is quite clear that in many instances what might have been tasteful design runs amok; barley-sugar twist supports, fret cutting, over carving and shaped edges have produced little more than ornate dust traps.

The nineteenth century saw many changes in attitude towards the furniture of the previous century. The work of Chippendale and Adam was often reviled, and it is not until the latter half of the century that eighteenth-century styles returned to favour. It began in the 1860's with a so-called 'Queen Anne revival' – many small kidney-shaped desks belong to this period – though even at this stage the Gothic of Pugin had still by no means disappeared from favour. At the Paris Exhibition in 1867 a satinwood cabinet in the Adam style was exhibited by Messrs Wright and Mansfield. The cabinet work was superb and it signalled a reappraisal of the eighteenth century. The use of jasper plaques in the decoration of this piece encouraged the use of ceramic mounts in English furniture, although the principal boost for this style of decoration originated in the 1862 Exhibition when many nineteenth-century reproductions of the Louis XV period were shown. Inlay had a great vogue in the middle of the century, not only in carefully chosen woods, but in ivory, mother-of-pearl and various marbles. Many Florentine mosaics were brought to England for table tops. Inlaid walnut cabinets became important features in many drawing rooms; the bow-fronted glazed display cabinet usually described today as a 'vitrine', is one of the kinds typical of the 1860's. Low cabinets, either closed or open, were in great demand and some of the most beautiful at this time, restrained in their design and delightfully proportioned as well as being useful pieces of furniture, were those made by Gillow and Company.

Vitrine or china display cabinet.

After 1870 furniture takes on even greater 'weight'. It was as though the Italian Renaissance had happened quite recently and its symbolism had rapidly invaded the work of the leading designers. In England it became known as the 'free Renaissance' and the cabinet furniture at this time expresses it best. Dark rosewood and ebonised cabinets, sideboards and overmantels were carved and inlaid, and the use of engraved ivory as an inlay was perhaps the most popular of all. Carved wood panels abounded and some of the best work in this field was carried out by the firm of Collinson and Lock, who were taken over by Gillows in 1894. To the late twentieth-century eye the 'free Renaissance' looks extremely odd and it is somewhat difficult to give it the appreciation that it earned when Robert Edis published his *Furniture and Decoration of Town Houses* in 1880. The 'free Renaissance' has been described by one critic as the 'bracket and overmantel style', and nothing could describe the period more perfectly.

Influential Victorians

Sir Charles Barry (1795–1860), architect. After travelling in Europe and Asia Minor he made major sketching expeditions to Egypt and Palestine. He designed churches and a number of other buildings in London such as the Reform Club in Pall Mall, probably his finest work. While engaged in work on King Edward VI's Grammar School at Birmingham he met A. W. Pugin and John Thomas who were to support him so well during his rebuilding of the Houses of Parliament. The Houses of Parliament burned down in 1834, and the new buildings, which were ordered to be built in 'Gothic or Elizabethan', were opened in 1852 by Queen Victoria. Barry was knighted shortly afterwards. Barry later established schools of modelling, stone and wood carving and cabinet making.

William Butterfield (1814–1900), architect. He began his architectural education at Worcester where a sympathetic head clerk with archaeological tastes and interests encouraged him in the study of English medieval building, which was to lay the foundation of his future career. He designed a number of churches, including All Saints, Margaret Street, London, and new buildings at Merton College, Oxford; he was also the designer of Keble College, Oxford, which was founded in 1870.

Astley Paston Cooper (1768–1841), President of the College of Surgeons and Fellow of the Royal Society. Cooper was one of the leading surgeons of the day and during his work at Guy's Hospital he became extremely well known to the public. He was noted for his contacts with the resurrectionists of the period. He received a baronetcy following an operation he performed upon George IV. In one year his income was £21,000. His name has become well known to those involved in furniture design through his invention of tall-back chairs to encourage the proper deportment of young people.

Owen Jones (1809–1874), architect and ornamental designer, born in London, the only son of a well-known Welsh antiquary. He studied at the Royal Academy and afterwards travelled extensively in Europe and the Middle East where he became deeply impressed with Arabic form and ornament. In 1851 he received the appointment of Superintendent of the Works of the Great Exhibition and was active in the overall decoration and arrangement. In his later years Owen Jones was employed extensively in the decoration of private houses and in 1857 received the Gold Medal of the Royal Institute of British Architects. He published several important volumes on design and his *Grammar of Ornament* which appeared in 1856 had considerable influence on the designs of English wallpapers, carpets and furniture.

Augustus Welby Pugin (1812–1852), architect and writer. He was the son of A. C. Pugin who trained him in architecture and from whom he inherited great skill as a draughtsman. Although his life was so brief, Pugin produced a vast quantity of work and, as well as the important buildings which he carried out, his publications had far-reaching influence. In 1841 his *True Principles of Pointed or Christian Architecture* did much to further the Gothic interests of the day and, in the field of furniture design, encouraged among Victorians the idea that there was a built-in morality connected simply with the presence of Gothic furniture in the house. In 1851 he was appointed a Commissioner of Fine Arts for the Great Exhibition, but before the year was out his mind was to break under the strain and in 1852 he was removed to Bedlam.

Anthony Salvin (1799–1881), architect. Born at Worthing; on completing his education at Durham School he entered the office of John Nash. In due course he became recognised as the greatest authority on medieval military architecture and he carried out major works at the Tower of London. His work in restoring manor houses and the building of country seats in many parts of Britain very much affected the contemporary fashions in interior design.

Henry Shaw (1800–1873), architectural draughtsman, engraver and antiquary. He supplied most of the illustrations of Wells and Gloucester Cathedrals for John Britton's famous *Cathedral Antiquaries of England*. He produced a number of volumes on ornament that proved to be of great value to furniture designers in the middle of the nineteenth century. These are: *Examples of Ornamental Metal Work*, 1836; *Specimens of Ancient Furniture*, 1836; *Ancient Plate and Furniture from the Colleges of Oxford and the Ashmolean Museum*, 1837; and *Specimens of the Details of Elizabethan Architecture*, 1839. His *Encyclopaedia of Ornament* appeared in 1842.

John Thomas (1813–1862), sculptor and architectural draughtsman. He was first apprenticed to a stone mason and later he assisted his brother William, the architect, at Birmingham. He came to the notice of Sir Charles Barry whose interest had been aroused by a monument executed by Thomas. During the rebuilding of the Houses of Parliament he was engaged by Barry to work on the sculptural decorations of the new structure and subsequently he took charge of the entire labour force engaged on this particular work. The colossal lions at the ends of the Britannia Bridge over the Menai Straits are a characteristic example of his work.

10
The Movement Forward

William Morris

In 1880 Karl Marx's *Das Kapital* was published in English translation and in the same year Trade Union membership topped half a million; two years later someone tried to shoot the Queen and in 1884 the Third Reform Bill was passed, giving the vote to virtually every householder in the country. To many prosperous Victorians – employers and property-owners – it must have seemed that the Socialist state was at hand and revolution only just around the corner. But in fact the early socialists in England were not revolutionaries; they were middle-class intellectuals – like the Webbs, Arnold Toynbee, Bernard Shaw and William Morris – who devoted their lives to the working-class movement because their sense of justice was sickened by the misery and ugliness of the industrial slums. They dreamed of a world where men had 'employment that would foster their self-respect . . . and lived in surroundings that would soothe and elevate them. There is only one thing that can give them this,' said Morris, 'and that is Art.' It was the deadening effects of mass-production, the slavery to the machine that bred the ugliness, the debased designs and the still more debased lives of the industrial age. England, he believed, must return to peasant communities and hand craftsmanship if she was to be saved. And although it was a bit late in the day to re-organise the whole of society on these lines, Morris did succeed in founding a movement which changed the course of English design and had a far-reaching influence abroad.

He was born in 1834 and spent his boyhood on the edge of Epping Forest, a landscape that taught him to understand growing things and wild creatures and to love the countryside. It was there he first began to read the medieval poetry and romance that became one of his passions. At school at Marlborough and later at Oxford he studied the history of the Middle Ages and came to know and love early Gothic buildings; he abandoned his early plan to take Orders and decided to become an architect instead. In the event, he became a designer, a painter, a poet, a weaver, a political thinker and a manufacturer.

Dining chair by Morris, Marshall, Faulkner and Co.

In 1861 Morris founded the firm of Morris, Marshall, Faulkner & Co., which he described as 'a Company of historical artists'. The seven partners included the Pre-Raphaelite painters Burne-Jones and Rossetti, whose outlook and ideals had much in common with Morris's own. This was the beginning of a movement which produced a number of good designers and provided the background for some of the best work of the years that followed; its motto might well have been Morris's own guiding principle: 'Have nothing in your house that you do not know to be useful or believe to be beautiful.' It was his belief that civilisation had taken a wrong turning at the end of the Middle Ages and that it was necessary to return to medieval principles before a new way forward could be found. As he grew older he tempered his views a little; it was not essential to adopt wholesale the arts and crafts of the Middle Ages; even machines might sometimes have their uses; in a lecture he called 'How we live and how we might live', he said:

> If the necessary reasonable work be of a mechanical kind, I must be helped to do it by a machine, not to cheapen my labour, but so that as little time as possible may be spent on it, and that I may be able to think of other things while I am tending the machine.

One of the most active members of Morris's firm was Philip Webb (1831–1915). Although he was primarily an architect – he served his articles in Reading – he produced designs of the most varied kinds for the firm and his furniture was particularly distinctive and practical. He also build some fine houses and made some very successful additions to old buildings. He was, incidentally, typical of Morris's followers in refusing to undertake any work that he was unable to supervise himself.

One of the first products of the firm had been wallpaper, some of it designed by Burne-Jones; in 1875 Morris became the sole proprietor of the firm and he then turned his attention to dyeing and weaving and became an expert in both. His beautiful fabrics had a great success in the fashionable world and did much to spread the fame of his ideas. His designs were based on a study of nature which, he believed, should be the direct model for the artist; it was the symbolism of the organic forces of the plant which became one of the sources of inspiration for the Art Nouveau movement.

Although Morris never made – and probably never even designed – any furniture himself, his views on craftsmanship and on functional simplicity made radical changes in English furniture design. The beauty of any object, he believed, depended on the suitability of its design to its purpose and on the craftsmanship of its maker. Anything made for merely ornamental purposes would be a failure. The ill-conceived decoration to be seen in the catalogues of commercial manufacturers was the result of ignoring this principle. A farm-cart, said Morris, was not designed to be decorative; but it was a beautiful object because it was made by craftsmen with a practical purpose in mind. His own firm made a chair which provides an excellent example of his methods. It is rush-seated, with an ebonised beech frame and supports, and was adapted from a traditional country chair from Sussex. These chairs originally sold for five shillings each.

The Arts and Crafts movement

The movement that had started in Morris's firm soon gathered momentum; there were many of his contemporaries, particularly among the young and the better educated, who found much to dislike not only in the hideous results of mass-production but in the society that fostered it. They were anxious to return to what they conceived to be the values and virtues of an older and simpler way of life. They became some of Morris's most ardent disciples; even their dress followed his principles. In an age of formal tailoring and stiff collars, the men wore loose jackets and flowing cravats; the women renounced bustles, tight lacing and wasp-waists and copied the graceful simplicity of Burne-Jones's ladies. They gave up the complicated rituals of Victorian Society and retired to the country to make pottery and read Swinburne.

Groups of craftsmen – both amateur and professional – began to come together in what was almost a revival of the medieval Guild system; their ideals were simplicity of design and the highest possible standards of craftsmanship. They took pleasure in timber for its own sake; they would often make no attempt to conceal the methods used in construction – dowels and the various means of jointing were deliberately used as decoration. One of the most important of these groups was the Cotswold School whose members shared a passionate interest in traditional country-made furniture. They were among the most avant-garde designers of the day and worked strictly to William Morris principles. Among the most important of them were Sidney and Ernest Barnsley, Ernest Gimson, William Lethaby and Reginald Blomfield; Gimson and the Barnsleys were the founders of the group, who first set up a workshop in the Cotswold Hills not far from Cirencester.

Much of their furniture does possess a rustic air; they achieved the somewhat austere appearance for which it is noted by the considerable use of frame and panel construction. As in early Gothic chest furniture, wrought iron frequently provided the decoration – showing the hammer blows as much as possible in order to emphasise the hand-made nature of the product. Even houses were constructed in a similar manner using pegged timbers and hand-made iron nails.

There was also a passion for painting furniture and, again, it was derived from thirteenth-century Gothic originals. In the 1862 Exhibition such pieces were prominent, including the well-known 'St George Cabinet' designed by Philip Webb. Much furniture was painted in pale colours – particularly green – and ebonised woods were also very much sought after. On some of the painted cabinets and wardrobes painted leather panels, tooled and gilded, were added as a decoration.

Art Nouveau

Many English designers became deeply involved in the creation of European Art Nouveau. It was A. H. Mackmurdo (1851–1942), founder of the Century Guild in 1882, who first drew ornament in furniture that is undoubtedly Art Nouveau. He used a lot of oak in construction and many of his designs are characterised by their capping with what amounts to a classical cornice. Even in his smaller items his furniture shows a deeply satisfying architectural unity. There are exceptions however, and a mahogany chair of his, of 1882, with an Art Nouveau painted fretwork in the form of swirling seaweeds, while retaining brilliance as an example of early Art Nouveau, does not possess unity as a whole.

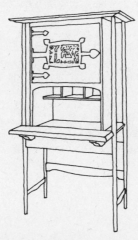

Oak writing desk with brass fittings and hinges. Designed by C. F. A. Voysey, 1896.

Charles Francis Annesley Voysey was remarkable among the designers of English Art Nouveau. He achieved a considerable reputation on the Continent and yet he was almost insular in his disregard of Continental productions. His entire output was constructed in plain oak. He saw simplicity as the key to interior decoration and he used such items of metal as locks and hinges to provide ornament. Voysey's use of cornice tops or square finials was clearly borrowed from Mackmurdo's designs, while his use of pictorial copper hinges was very much his own. A good deal of British Art Nouveau owes a debt to Bruce Talbert, a designer who, in 1867, had published a volume under the title *Gothic Forms Applied to Furniture*. He too had employed frame and panel construction but had used inlaid geometrical patterns or carved panels for decoration. He also encouraged the use of Gothic-style strap hinges in gilt metal. Talbert produced designs for Gillows and for Holland and Son. Another important progressive designer was Charles Lock Eastlake; his book *Hints on*

Household Taste, published in 1868, proclaimed a return to simpler and cheaper interior designs, and it greatly encouraged more popular interest in and demand for what was known as Art Furniture.

Art Nouveau takes its name from a shop in Paris opened in 1895 by Samuel Bing, which he called L'Art Nouveau. It is a style that has many diverse roots: the Gothic and Celtic revivals; the drawings of William Blake; the pre-Raphaelite movement; the Arts and Crafts movement; French poster art and – among the most significant – the art of Japan. The use of a flowing line and a broad mass of colour, as used in the Japanese woodblock print, made a great impact on European designers; this had been reinforced by the popularity of the Japanese wares Bing imported for his shop. In England the interest in Japanese styles dated back to the Exhibition of 1862. This exhibition owed much of its success to the work of Arthur Lasenby Liberty who had a great interest in Oriental art and who was in charge of the arrangement of the Japanese exhibits. When he opened his famous shop in 1875 his stock strongly reflected Art Nouveau styles and the very word 'Liberty' became associated with them.

One of the most distinguished British exponents of Art Nouveau was the architect Charles Rennie Mackintosh, a dominant figure of the Glasgow school. He was perhaps the most revolutionary British architect of the late nineteenth century and in his furniture design he achieved some of the most elegant and sophisticated examples of the period. He owed enough to the Arts and Crafts movement to resist the overflow of ornament that was coming to dominate European art and his furniture, particularly his cabinets, are distinguished for their beautiful balance and their somewhat elongated and asymmetrical form.

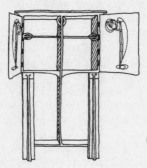

C. R. Mackintosh cabinet on stand.

Edward Godwin

Edward William Godwin (1833–1886) was also an architect. His most celebrated building was Whistler's White House, Tite Street, Chelsea. During the 1860's he became interested in furniture design and, in particular, he developed a remarkable affinity with Japanese furniture; in fact much of his work is frequently termed 'Anglo-Japanese'. While the Japanese-inspired examples of Godwin's work are well known, it would be quite wrong to believe that Japanese art was his only study. He did travel extensively, but never to the Far East, and his notebooks – now in the collections of the Victoria and Albert Museum – show his interest in Greek sources as well as Egyptian ornament, illuminated manuscripts and Gothic and Renaissance architecture. His interest in simple shapes was first aroused when he moved his architectural practice to London in 1867, and made a discovery:

> When I came to furniture I found that hardly anything could be bought ready made that was at all suitable to the requirements of the case. I therefore set to work and designed a lot of furniture and with a desire for economy directed it to be made of deal ebonised. There were no mouldings, no ornamental work and no carving. Such effect as I wanted, I endeavoured to gain as in economical building, by the grouping of solid and void and by more or less broken outline.

It was a revolutionary idea, and went further even than Morris, Marshall, Faulkner & Co., most of whose products were heavily painted. Godwin's error was in using deal which proved an unsatisfactory economy and resulted in his having his furniture remade in mahogany, although he still carried through his original plan and had the pieces ebonised. His philosophy was simple and to the point. As he wrote:

> It is easy enough to make furniture in direct imitation of any particular style, especially the old English styles, with such Museums as that at Kensington open to us. What I have endeavoured to secure in design, has rather been a modern treatment of certain well known and admired styles than a mere reproduction of old forms.

Such pieces were in anticipation of much of the Art Nouveau of the 1890's. Some of his furniture actually included carved boxwood insets from Japan and Japanese ivory handles. It is virtually certain that much of his knowledge of Japanese furnishings derived from the collection of Japanese colour prints in the possession of a friend of his named William Burges. Burges's main interest however, as an architect and furniture designer, was in medieval themes.

Godwin set out to eliminate unnecessary detail but he always had an understanding eye for innovations that might suit particular styles. He saw in Arthur Lasenby Liberty's new shop some Japanese embossed wallpaper which closely resembled leather and he realised at once that such papers could well be used for filling the otherwise plain panels of cheaper furniture – which he did with great success.

Godwin's furniture is, first and foremost, functional; his interest in style was secondary and although he might claim that various of his pieces belonged to particular periods or countries, this is not always immediately obvious from their design. His armchair in the 'Jacobean' style, with its circular cane seat and slender plain supports, produces very little sense of the seventeenth century; his 'Greek' chairs do not look noticeably Greek and his furniture in the 'English manner' somehow contrives to look Oriental. But his achievements in functional design are a clear signpost to much of what is best in twentieth-century furniture development. Godwin worked closely with William Watt of

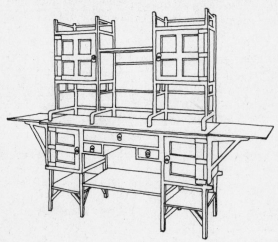

Sideboard by E. W. Godwin in ebonised mahogany with silver-plated hinges and handles. It is influenced by Japanese forms and the panels are filled with Liberty's embossed Japanese leather paper. Designed in 1867.

Grafton Street in London – an excellent cabinet maker who described himself as an 'art furniture maker'. He also produced designs for important firms of furniture manufacturers, such as Green & King and Messrs Gillow; and he was paid a retainer by Collinson & Lock. His work was quite often copied – rather badly – by other manufacturers and his ideas gained wide currency on the Continent.

Wallpapers

Wallpaper came to fill a major role in late Victorian interior design. Many furnishers even covered panels of interior doors with it. The old principle of the unity of a room and its contents was again the vogue, and Victorian fashion placed great emphasis on a relationship between wallpaper and furniture. Earlier A. W. Pugin had produced wallpaper designs; now the stylised floral motifs of William Morris and his colleagues often formed the ideal background to the late nineteenth-century room decorated in the Art Nouveau manner.

Wall coverings, other than wood panelling, had been considered in terms of decoration at a much earlier date. Block-printed wallpaper was known in England from the early sixteenth century and leather wall coverings were not unusual in houses decorated during the reign of William and Mary. Oriental and Oriental-style wallpapers were of course fashionable during the periods of the main Chinoiserie enthusiasms. An example of the relationship between such paper and Oriental furnishing can best be seen at the Royal Pavilion, Brighton.

Victorian wallpapers often added to the general sense of over-furnishing in many Victorian interiors. At the turn of the century some particularly tasteless wallpapers evolved and this was, no doubt, largely responsible for the reaction in the twentieth century when wallpaper went largely out of fashion and paint took its place. Indeed in the period immediately following the Second World War there was even considerable antipathy towards hanging pictures.

New techniques

During the second half of the nineteenth century bentwood furniture became popular in England. An Austrian, Michael Thonet, developed chairs that were cheap, strong, light and elegant, but unfortunately – as with all products where mass-production is possible – bentwood furniture rapidly became mediocre and soon found itself relegated to the public house rather than the drawing room. The bentwood rocking chair, however, frequently ebonised, is a design that has great beauty and was undoubtedly a revealing glimpse into the future. In due course Thonet opened showrooms in London. The timber used in the bentwood productions was shaped in steam presses and was therefore in complete contrast to traditional joinery. It is really only in this twentieth century that Thonet's revolutionary designs have been credited with the importance they deserve.

Early bentwood rocking chair from designs by Thonet.

At the end of the nineteenth century the new veneer cutting machines and, in particular the rotary slicer, encouraged a minor revolution. It was not that the cost of veneers was not now quite reasonable – they were cheap. But the new machines minimised waste and the thin veneers could be formed into a three-layer sandwich that was both strong and light. It was the beginning of plywood construction on a big scale and it now became possible for large flush areas such as wardrobe doors to be veneered in rare wood. With solid timber there is either swelling or shrinkage in the width of the grain, but with plywood there are no such problems. It was found that it could also be moulded to shape and with the use of new glues jointing could also be eliminated. Such discoveries opened new avenues of furniture design, while at the same time creating dismay among those cabinet makers who worshipped permanently at the altar of Chippendale.

These new techniques, however, did not mean that traditional methods of construction were to be forgotten; but modern designers were now finding new opportunities to exploit new ideas.

11
The Twentieth Century

Ambrose Heal

During the reign of Edward VII Art Nouveau continued to exert a strong influence on interior design; there was also a great demand for reproductions of antique furniture, both French and English. But some of the best furniture of the period was made by the Cotswold School. The Arts and Crafts Society, which William Morris had founded in 1888, gave regular exhibitions which did much to encourage good design and higher standards of craftsmanship and the work of Ernest Gimson and the Barnsleys continued to foster the enthusiasm for traditional English furniture.

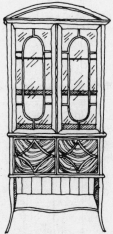

Edwardian display cabinet. Much Edwardian cabinet work is of very high quality and many of the most popular designs are clearly derived from Sheraton.

The Windsor chair has an apparently perennial appeal – it is still in demand today – but in the early years of this century the ladder-back chairs made by the Cotswold craftsmen were almost

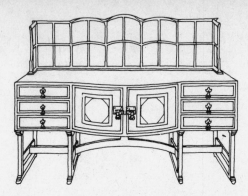

Sideboard by Ernest Gimson in walnut with the back rail, feet and stretchers in ebony.

equally popular. Gimson had been taught chair-making by Clisset of Bosbury, in Herefordshire, and his rush-seated ladder-back chairs and those by C. F. A. Voysey are superb examples of advanced peasant design. The lessons of William Morris – and in particular his insistence that designers should have a thorough knowledge of their materials and that they should be workmen as well as draughtsmen – had not been forgotten; they were perpetuated in the work of the Cotswold School and they had their influence on the next generation of designers as well.

Ambrose Heal, one of the most outstanding designers of the new generation, had been trained as a cabinet maker and, what was more, he belonged to the furniture trade; his family had one of the best established businesses in London. Heal's furniture, unlike that of the Cotswold School, was intended for commercial manufacture and was therefore designed to produce a proper relationship between the work of the machine and the work of the craftsman. He liked plain symmetrical lines which displayed the timber he used to the best advantage and his decoration was limited to inlay, moulded drawer edges and circular or oval panels. He also made sunken handles an integral part of his designs so that the characteristic outline of his furniture is smooth and unbroken. Heal's simple and highly functional style was copied and adapted by many other designers and manufacturers and set a trend which was still being followed in the twenties and thirties. Plain kitchen dressers, cupboards and tables, rush-seated chairs and Heal's bedroom furniture probably represent the best designs of the early twentieth century.

Cross-currents from overseas

From the very first, the Arts and Crafts Society had made quite as much impact abroad as it made in England; and the ideals of the Cotswold School, based as they were on traditional design, found a ready response in Austria and in Germany. They even spread to the United States where they were taken up by the architect Frank Lloyd Wright.

Chaise longue.

The growth of advertising and of photography meant that new movements in design spread more rapidly than ever before and there was a cross-fertilisation between the fashions of Europe and the States as well as between those of Britain and the Continent. The changes in chair design, for example, between the 1860's and the 1920's provide an interesting commentary on this exchange of ideas. The shapes range from the early bentwood chairs of Michael Thonet to those of Frank Lloyd Wright; and from the tubular steel and canvas of Breuer and the moulded plywood of the American Charles Ray Eames to the more conventional designs of E. Rimaldi. In 1926 Mies van der Rohe made the first cantilevered chair, in which the legs were replaced by a tubular metal support; and in 1929 he produced his Barcelona chair, which was first shown at the International Exhibition held in that city. It has been described as 'perhaps the

Barcelona chair.

most beautiful modern chair' and is still being manufactured today both in Europe and America.

One of the most influential designers in Germany was Professor Walter Gropius, the director of the Bauhaus School of Design in Weimar. The ideas of the Bauhaus Group were already beginning to spread through Europe and America in the twenties and had had a profound effect on avant-garde architecture as well as on most other forms of design. With the rise of the Third Reich however, all modern developments in the arts came to an abrupt halt and the Bauhaus School was forcibly closed down. In the thirties Gropius and his fellow teachers emigrated and their views gained even wider currency, particularly in America where experiments in furniture design made the American industry a focal point for the rest of the Western world. Some of Gropius's innovations continue to influence furniture manufacture even today – notably his superb unit furniture which dates from the 1920's.

One of the disciples of Walter Gropius who made his way to England during the thirties was Marcel Breuer, who had been engaged on some interesting experiments in laminated wood; he continued these in London and produced some bentwood furniture that contributed to the revival of its popularity. His bent plywood stacking tables were the forerunners of much of the cheap stacking furniture of our own times.

The 'Wassily' chair designed by Marcel Breuer in 1925. The first tubular steel chair.

Sir Gordon Russell

Between the wars there was a vast expansion in house-building – some of it 'ribbon development' on an immense scale and some of it in the form of detached dwellings in the now ubiquitous mock-Tudor – 'stockbrokers' Tudor' – which was favoured in the more prosperous suburbs. These houses were very often furnished in a deplorable version of mock-Jacobean which became extremely popular during the twenties and goes far to establish the claim that this period was the 'dark age' of English furniture. At the same time, the mushroom growth of smaller, cheaper houses was creating its own demand for mass-produced furniture and the introduction of hire-purchase meant that manufacturers were in a position they had never been in before – they were faced with a market which they could not satisfy.

It was not only in supplying the mass market that the furniture trade fell short; there were still craftsmen, such as Gimson and Edward Barnsley, who made furniture by hand; but there were also designers – Heal, for example, and Gordon Russell – whose work was expressly planned for production by machine. The trouble was that at this time the machine was less sophisticated than the designs, and mechanisation could not rise to the new challenge.

The leader in British industrial design responsible for putting the partnership of machine and handwork into proper perspective was Gordon Russell. During World War II he became Chairman of the Design Panel at the Board of Trade which was to play such an important role in the national production of Utility furniture, and in 1947 he became Director of the Council of Industrial Design. After the first World War he had begun to design individual pieces of furniture at his home in the Cotswolds, like so many of the designers and craftsmen of the period. The Russell family had known many of them and it was the work of Ernest Gimson which had particularly influenced the furniture produced by the Russell family business.

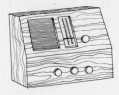

Radio cabinet designed by R. D. Russell for the firm of Gordon Russell.

Sir Gordon Russell's autobiography *Designer's Trade*, published in 1968, is full of clear insight into the twentieth century:

> I felt very strongly that my generation, which had destroyed so much lovely work, had a constructive duty to perform; somehow or other we had to hand on to those coming after us good things of our own creation. I was aware that a venture of this

sort, in which we would learn as we went along, would cost money, but there was money about and there was a great pent-up demand for goods of all kinds. My working knowledge of old furniture gave me a respect for tradition, which I believe to be most important if one wants to try to see today's work in perspective. To me it was a poor age which could make no contribution of its own. I argued that if the eighteenth century had been content to imitate the seventeenth, then the finest age of English cabinet making would never have been born. Further, it was my great love for old things which made me wish to design new ones: I had far too much respect for the past not to be revolted by the regurgitations I saw on all sides. I had no qualifications beyond a burning belief that my own age might recover its self-respect, a sound knowledge of old furniture and construction and an interest in the possibilities of the machine . . .

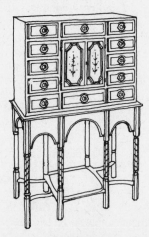

Cabinet in solid English walnut, inlaid with ebony, yew and box. Awarded gold medal at Paris Exhibition, 1925. Designer Gordon Russell. Cabinet maker William Marks.

Like the designers of the Cotswold School, Sir Gordon Russell believed that the artist must have an understanding of the work being done at the bench and equally that the craftsman must appreciate the importance of design; and like Heal he was very much aware that designs intended for machines required a very different approach from work designed for hand production. By the twenties, attitudes among the exponents of the two methods were hardening. Manufacturers considered the arts and crafts movement to be 'precious' and impractical, while the hand craftsmen denounced the machine as the enemy of all good design and decent workmanship.

What is important in machine production is the manner in which the machine is used. The fundamental problem was, and is, as Sir Gordon Russell has so clearly outlined:

> to use the machine in the best way for the work for which it was suitable, and to maintain a fine standard of handwork showing qualities which a machine could not give. It does not seem to have been clear to Morris that the machine had come to stay, because it alone made possible the production of ordinary things in sufficient quantity for everyone to be able to use them. He was annoyed, too, to find that his beautiful handmade things were expensive and could only be bought by people whose incomes came from the use of machinery.

In 1942 Dr Hugh Dalton, then President of the Board of Trade, arranged for the setting up of a committee to advise on the introduction of Utility furniture. Such furniture, available on coupons as it was wartime, began to appear in the shops early in 1943, and it was not subject to purchase tax. Furniture designers responsible for this important work were H. J. Cutler and Edwin Clinch of High Wycombe. Because of transport problems during the war such furniture could not be mass-produced in the normally accepted sense of the word: it had to be made in the area in which it was to be sold. The furniture was not always treated kindly by the Press – or indeed by the public – and there was much criticism of the use of hardboard for the backs of cupboards and the bottoms of drawers. The very word 'utility' came to mean shoddy and second rate; but while the manufacture of this furniture was a temporary wartime expedient, it may have had its uses as an experiment in design.

In 1945 Sir Gordon Russell was invited to sit on the Design Committee of the Furniture Trade Working Party, one of several set up to investigate conditions in various industries after the war, in order to make recommendations for improvement. The design section in the report of the Furniture Trade Working Party was drafted by Sir Gordon himself. At the time of publishing his autobiography – more than twenty years after the publication of the report – he could see no reason to alter his original summing up:

In the furniture industry design is so important that we have spent a considerable time investigating the position closely. In many industries, for example in the manufacture of aeroplanes, locomotives and many other technical products, it is the functional aspect of design which is of fundamental importance and though a certain beauty is often achieved, it is almost incidental. But in furniture the problem of design is not purely functional; furniture has to be lived with at close quarters and not only must it give efficient service, but it must also give pleasure. In our opinion, therefore, it is proper that this subject should occupy one of the most important parts of our report. We started by assuming that it would be generally accepted that there is such a thing as a standard of good design; that the industry has a responsibility to supply furniture of good quality, including quality of design; and that there is at present great scope for improvement. But our discussions have shown that this assumption is by no means common ground in the industry and that some firms would in fact strongly oppose it. We feel, therefore, that before proceeding to a detailed consideration of the problem of design we should state clearly the premises on which we have based our approach to it.

The idea that good design must satisfy a number of well-defined conditions has long been accepted by those who have made a study of it, but this idea is still so generally unfamiliar that we feel justified in outlining its necessary conditions. We believe that good industrial design is concerned with form, colour, decoration, texture, fitness for its job, method of production, method of transport and saleability. It is not something applied at the end nor is it something different for the sake of being different. Conscious design must start at the inception of the article and go on steadily till the end. It is in the early stages that the basic shapes and many details are fluid. An opportunity missed then will not recur, and it is only the trained and imaginative designer who is likely to be aware of its existence. Good industrial design under present-day conditions is the work of a group of technicians of whom the leader is the industrial designer. If properly trained he is the obvious person to express an opinion on function, form, colour, texture, finish, etc. He must work in the closest collaboration with the mill manager, sales manager and others. When a technically-minded artist has been stimulated by a problem he and his team will be likely to get the best attainable results out of the complicated industrial processes of today and the available materials, adapted to the ends which the object has to serve. For this reason it will be seen that good industrial design must of necessity be in tune with its own age. The copying of the forms of a past age which were designed for totally different conditions, materials and methods of production will get nowhere, whereas a knowledge of the past used as an inspiration for the future may be of real value. It is true to say that our heritage of furniture in this country is so fine that, if once we could find our way to the right road again, we might well become world leaders once more. We must learn again to think of design as an essential element of quality, as important as materials and workmanship.

It is essential that a well-designed object should not only do its job with he maximum efficiency; it should also give visual pleasure. People however have widely different views on what gives them visual pleasure. To know what one likes is not necessarily to know what is good and what will stand the test of time. Just as writing is complementary to reading, without which it would serve no use, so industrial design needs its public. And good industrial design needs a critical and appreciative public.

Any improvement in industrial design will increase the size of this public, already greater than many manufacturers and retailers believe, by making well-designed things more familiar to the mass of people. The interest aroused by excellent Service exhibitions, by cheap and good books, and by music should be borne in mind in this connection.

We must emphasize that whether industrial design is deemed good, bad or indifferent is not merely a matter of opinion. It is a matter on which all those who have a trained aesthetic sensibility the world over will agree, in broad principle. To say that they have no right to do this and that they speak with no more authority than, say a vagrant brought up in one of our great industrial towns is nonsense – such a man, it is likely, has never considered the problem and has hardly a single thing of beauty about him. It would be as reasonable to say that a man trained as an accountant is no more fit to air his views on book-keeping than an engine driver. We accept the view that a very large proportion of the furniture made in this country before the war was of poor design and we cannot say too strongly that we feel that the inhabitants of our industrial towns should not be fobbed off with ugly things because they live in squalid surroundings, and because for the moment many will accept such things as natural. An increasing number is aware that something is missing in their lives and the furniture trade would acquire immense prestige if it accepted the responsibility of becoming leader of the more forward-minded. Moreover, such an attitude is essential in export trade where competition, although much more severe than at home, is easier to deal with on a quality basis than a strictly price basis.

In 1951 – the centenary of Prince Albert's Great Exhibition – the Festival of Britain was inaugurated. It too showed the world all that was newest in British technology and design and although the style associated with it has not proved lastingly popular, it certainly aroused great interest in new building and new furniture, both in the public at large and in industry itself. This interest has been fostered by the Council of Industrial Design and kept alive through the Design Centre, which opened in the Haymarket in London, in 1956.

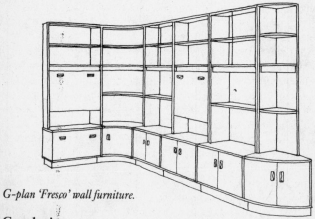

G-plan 'Fresco' wall furniture.

Conclusion

One of the paradoxical results of mass-production is the almost mystical value that now attaches to any object – lace or jewellery or glass or furniture – that has been made by hand. If any of the furniture of today is treasured, as the furniture of Chippendale or Hepplewhite was treasured, and handed on down the generations, it seems safe to assume that it will come not from a production line but from the workshop of one of the craftsmen still to be found in many parts of Britain, who are capable of making custom-built furniture of outstanding quality. It is to be hoped that for many years to come there will also be patrons with the discrimination and self-confidence to demand the best and the means to ensure that they get it. One notable twentieth-century example of such a patron was Sir Winston Churchill.

Churchill was always interested in design and in domestic comfort; he was particularly fond of library furniture and he also had strong views on the proper furnishing of a dining-room. At his old home at Chartwell in Kent, the white walls, unstained oak and green chintz in the dining room make a pleasant background for the breakfast and dining tables and the chairs which were all commissioned by the Churchills. Sir Winston took a close interest in their making and wrote a memorandum about the chairs which gets to the very heart of functional design:

> The Dining Room chair has certain very marked requisites. First, it should be comfortable and give support to the body when sitting up straight; it should certainly have arms, which are an enormous comfort when sitting at meals. Second, it should be compact. One does not want the Dining Room chair spreading itself, or its legs, or its arms, as if it were a plant, but an essentially upright structure with the arms and the back almost perpendicularly over the legs. This enables the chairs to be put close together if need be, which is often more sociable, while at the same time the arms prevent undue crowding and elbowing.

The dining chairs at Chartwell, made to a design by Winston Churchill.

After the General Election of 1945, Churchill decided to sell Chartwell; but a group of his friends, believing that the house was of historical importance, bought it and presented it to the National Trust on the understanding that Churchill might continue to live there for the rest of his life. After he died Lady

Churchill allowed most of the furniture to remain in the house; and Sir Winston's chairs are still in the dining-room.

Failing the kind of customer who commissions furniture to his own specifications, most of the craftsmen of today copy traditional designs; very few of them are capable of giving their work a distinctive identity in terms of style and the time has almost certainly gone when an individual cabinet maker could influence new developments. These must evolve – as they have so often evolved in the past – to meet new domestic needs and to keep pace with social change. High land values have resulted in smaller houses and a consequent demand for space-saving furniture such as built-in cupboards, multi-purpose wall units, bunk beds and retractable beds that double as sofas. Some houses have no dining-room, so a room-divider is installed in the living-room and a breakfast bar in the kitchen. The kitchen itself has been revolutionised; with its laminated plastic work-tops and storage units, its stainless steel and its electronic control panels – however admirably designed – the modern kitchen bears about as much relation to its traditional counterpart as a nuclear submarine to the Cutty Sark. And already its clinical austerity has produced a reaction and a return to stripped pine and checked gingham and rocking chairs by the kitchen range.

In the rest of the house the designers have served the scientists rather less well. When clocks and barometers became available in the late seventeenth century, the craftsmen of the day rose to the occasion and produced cases for them that were practical, beautiful and admirably suited to their purpose; the invention of radio and television and hi-fi has not met with a similar response. The designers have played safe – in England at least; they have assumed that if the products of modern technology must find a place in the living-room, they should, as far as possible, be concealed; and that since old styles signify good taste, the most suitable housing for television sets and music-centres must be 'Queen Anne' cabinets or military chests. A generation ago, a similar outlook resulted in the production of 'Adam' electric fires with imitation flames and pseudo-Georgian cocktail cabinets.

Twentieth-century versions – good, bad and indifferent – of all kinds of furniture, in designs varying from Tudor to Regency, are mass-produced on a vast scale; at the same time the interest in antique furniture is growing stronger than ever. Perhaps this tendency to cling to the past is understandable at a time when current styles are so quickly overtaken by changes in fashion.

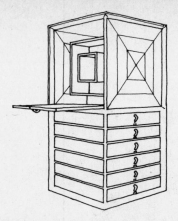

A double-sided desk for a husband and wife. The materials are Macassar ebony, holly, buffalo suede, Lebanon cedar and ivory. Designed and made by John Makepeace, FSIA, 1974.

The most important influence of recent years has been Scandinavian design which dominated the furniture – and of course the glass – of the sixties, both in Europe and America; this influence can still be seen at work today. But there have been others; every few months new trends sweep the world – from Brazil, or Italy or Japan – which are out of date almost before they are featured in the colour supplements. If there is to be any radical change – if any new style is to appear that will stamp its image on the furniture of the future with the authority of the great designers of the past – it seems inevitable that it must come not from the trend-setters but from technology itself; perhaps from the discovery of a new material or a new technique and from designers who have vision to exploit it creatively.

Appendix

Country furniture

A great quantity of furniture must have been constructed through many generations within the estates, villages and hamlets of England; but during the seventeenth and eighteenth centuries more and more furniture must have been sold to meet the demands of the countryside through fairs and markets. The inventories of household effects of the eighteenth century, and the wills of villagers and yeoman farmers indicate how much importance was set upon household goods of all kinds. The cottage interior is unlikely to have changed to any marked degree from one generation to the next, and it is for this reason that there has always been a wealth of good country furniture in Britain – an accumulation of riches that has never been given the appreciation and importance it deserves by the public at large or by successive governments who might well have considered steps to safeguard it.

Mendlesham chair. Daniel Day was a wheelwright of Mendlesham, Suffolk, who also made stick-back chairs. His son Richard later came to admire the designs of Thomas Sheraton, and together the Days produced this interesting hybrid. Early 19th century.

The regional variations in country furniture are of great interest. Marked differences occur, for example, between ladder-back chairs; while the Mendlesham chair is unique among provincial designs. Many of the country designs are original to their place of manufacture, and, contrary to popular belief, country furniture is by no means confined to unsophisticated interpretations of the fashionable styles of Chippendale and Hepplewhite.

Elm was used considerably by the country furniture maker, particularly in the production of seats for chairs. The primary reason for this was that elm could be worked very easily with the adze and would seldom split. Some of the most comfortable seats of saddle-form were manufactured in this manner and give complete comfort without upholstery or cushion. A number of eighteenth- and early nineteenth-century solid seat dining chairs, however, do have a low edge encircling the seat in order to accommodate a squab cushion. Spindle-back chairs, the product of the turner, are particularly associated with the North of England, most of them originating in Lancashire. The ladder-back chair, with various forms of seat, was popular throughout the country. Very often such chairs were stained, but others were kept 'in the white', the owners scouring them regularly with sand.

One of several traditional Windsor chair designs.

The Windsor chair is certainly the most celebrated country chair of all, and it is historically important as being the first example of furniture to use bentwood in its construction. The origin of the name Windsor is unknown, but there is a documentary reference to chairs of this name as early as 1725. It is possible that the main centre of production was in Buckinghamshire where large woodlands were available to provide the raw material and among the major owners of woodland in that country was a family named Windsor. In other parts of Britain, particularly in the West, it became known as a stick-back chair and other variations are described as comb-back. Later examples are frequently seen with a baluster-shaped central splat with pierced wheel cut design. The Windsor chair is probably the most timeless example of English furniture. Various woods have been used in its construction, some examples incorporating all four principal English timbers: elm, beech, oak and ash. While elm was favoured for the seat, the U-shaped hoop was normally made from ash. In the twentieth century collectors of country furniture have been particularly attracted by Windsor chairs constructed entirely in yew wood; the colour is undoubtedly warm and attractive and achieves a very fine polish. Consequently these chairs have now become rather costly. During the nineteenth century the simple elm cottage chair, with its vertical splats, became the most common chair in England, although, once again, it is interesting to see how sets of these are being assembled for use in the late twentieth-century dining-room. As mentioned earlier, the first version of the Windsor chair originated in the late seventeenth century; its design at that time would have held no appeal to the cabinet makers, but for the carpenter it was the perfect model on which to practise his skill. So popular did this chair become that many examples were shipped to America and, as a result, a number of American variations were made.

Most country communities had their chair-bodger, a man who in the main worked in the beech woods producing all turned sections for chairs. Chair-bodgers normally worked in pairs, one to supply the timber, the other to operate the pole-lathe and, while they are particularly associated with the Chilterns, they were in fact widely distributed through the country. The pole-lathe is a highly effective yet remarkably primitive tool, almost certainly being the oldest device for turning timber. Unlike the continuous action of a wheel-lathe, the pole-lathe takes its power from a springy pole or young tree. The operator uses a treadle that is connected by a rope to the top of the tree or pole, while the rope is twisted once around the piece of timber to be turned; therefore, when the treadle is depressed against the spring of the pole, force is generated causing the wood to turn, enabling shaping or other decoration to be carried out. By this method score after score of accurately aligned chair legs could be produced.

Unusual pieces of furniture are encountered from time to time. The bacon cupboard is one of them; although termed a cupboard, the immediate impression is that of a high backed settle. The seat itself is often fitted with a hinged top, or may have a base that is fitted with drawers. The tall back, often about six feet high, is in reality a very shallow cupboard with doors set into it. It was in these cupboards that the flitches of bacon were stored. Although such cupboards are curiosities they did not make comfortable seats and, as home curing became less common and the cottager or yeoman sought greater comfort, many such cupboards must have been destroyed or drastically converted to other uses.

Oak dresser, of which there were many regional variations.

The dresser is perhaps the best-known example of cottage furniture but, once again, there are many regional variations, and their development stretches from medieval times to the present day. The dresser as it is recognised today developed at about the same time as the Windsor chair, and the tall dresser backs with their rack of shelves have been a boon to collectors of country pottery ever since. In the medieval period the dresser was no more than a board on which to stand cups, the original cupboard. In important dwellings such cup-boards were developed in tiers, thus resulting in the early court cupboard or buffet; at the lower end of the social scale the simple board developed cupboards and drawers, and during the seventeenth century some very splendid examples were being produced. The back-board, with its moulded top, reached its first main period of development in the final decade of the seventeenth century and, like the long-case clock, the dresser, displaying its cargo of homely, decorated wares, was to become an object of affection in cottage and farm. Many such dressers were made in North Wales and the term Welsh dresser is well known. By no means all country-made dressers came from this area and when cross-banded or with inlay, they are much more likely to have emanated from the North of England.

Most homes at the end of the seventeenth century would have contained a clothes press or clothes cupboard; these spacious double-doored cupboards vary greatly in workmanship and choice of timber, although during the reign of Elizabeth I we find excellent examples in oak. Cupboards of this kind were a considerable progression from the chest, being far more convenient to use and enabling the contents to be aired conveniently. Many styles of hanging corner cupboards were to be found in the English cottage, and a variety of woods was used, lacquered examples being particularly attractive. Quite frequently lacquered furniture was painted over at a later date, in the same way that much good pine furniture was hidden under coats of chocolate brown or dark green. Very few of the old hanging corner cupboards found today date from before the middle of the eighteenth century.

Three-legged tables are still to be found in country dwellings, and are often exceedingly difficult to date, but they must owe their beginning to the same uneven floors that had prompted the three-legged stool. Gate leg tables, mentioned earlier in the book, were widely made in the English countryside; these folding tables, with their interesting grouping of gates and legs, particularly when well turned, have strong visual appeal. This attraction has ensured their manufacture down to the present day and there are many examples, therefore, which purport to be old yet, upon careful examination, prove not to be so. Again, it is worth mentioning that all stained furniture should be viewed with great care, as in most cases the stain will have been applied to simulate age in a far more recent specimen. Occasionally a band of carving may be seen applied close to the edge of such tables; invariably this will be found, if the table is old, to have been applied long after its original construction. The best examples of folding tables of all kinds will have a carefully produced rule-joint.

A variation of the gate leg table is the nineteenth-century Sutherland table with its narrow top and broad flaps. Even at the height of the Victorian era English country furniture maintained its appeal among those who sought straightforward, pleasing lines.

Extracts from farm and cottage inventories

Elizabeth Eree of Writtle, widow. 6 March 1705/6.

In the Hall – One longe table, six joyned stooles, one table leafe, a press cupboard & falling table att the end and earthen ware upon the cupbords heads, a livery table, an old skreene, a glass-case with the implements, a joyned forme, four old chaires, three spitts, three paire of pothooks, four paire of cobirons, two trammells and iron barr, a fender, a gridiron, a paire of bellows, & other implements, 2li. 10s.

In the parlour – One bedstead, curtaines, valents and rods, one feather bed and bolster and pillow, a pair of blankets, one rugg, bedmatt and cords, one press cupboard, a livery table, a falling table, two glasscases and implements, two looking glasses, two chaires, two stooles, one paire of bellows, and a candle box, & other implements, three window curtaines, & two rodds, 4li. 12s. 6d.

In the great buttrey – Three beere vessells, two beerstalls, one table, one swill tub, and other wooden & earthen ware, one brass copper, two brass kettles, a bras pann, and two bras pottage potts, a brass cullender, a skimmer, a warming pan, a coale dish, three skillets, two ladles, a brass potlid, a brass scone, one iron dripping pan, an iron pott & potthooke, one lanthorne, three tinn pans, & other implements, 3li. 3s. 10d.

In the little buttrey – Nine pewter dishes, one pewter bason, two plates, two porringers, two saucers, seaven pewter spoones, two pewter tankards, two pewter candlesticks, a candle cup, a flagon, a pewter cup, two salts, one frying pan, halfe a dozen plate trenchers, a drink stall, one powdring tub, earthen ware, & other implements, 1li. 1s. 7d.

In the chamber over the parlour – One feather bed, bolster and pillow, one blankett, one rugg, one quilt, one bedsted, curtaines, valents and rods, one table, two joyned stooles, two chaires, two large chests, two trunks, three boxes, one cabinett, 4li. 18s.

In the midle chamber – Three large chests, a nest of drawers, one armed chaire, and other odd things, 6s. 4d.

In the little chamber – A trundle bedsted, a straw bed, a flock bolster, and two matts, a needing trough, and a long forme, and other lumber, 8s. 4d.

In the chamber over the hall – A paire of wooden scales and beame, a side bed, one sack, one bagg, a peck and a halfe peck, one old horse baskett, a paire of winch pins, and other odd things, 3s. 2d.

In the wood house – Three tubs, a tunnell, a ladder, and other lumber, 12s. 6d.

Linnen – three paire of sheets, fifteen napkins, & one table cloth, 1li. 17s. 6d.

Wearing apparell and ready money, 2li.

The total sume is 2li. 13s. 9d.

(Appraisers – Christopher Lingard, John Hubbard.)

Robert Hilliard of Writtle, yeoman. 28 April 1708.

In the Hall – One long table, 4 joynt stools, 5 chaires rush ones, 1 payer of tongs, one fire shovell, 2 cobirons, one salt box, one payer of bellows, one chaffing dish, one warming pann, 2 spitts, one payer of tongs, one grid-iron, one clever, one lock iron, one pudding pann, one pessell and morter, 4 candle sticks, one glas casse, one candle sticke, one iron peall with small implyments, 1 li.

In the brewhouse and buttery – One copper, 2 pottig potts, 4 skillitt, one frying pann, two bras kettles, one hodgsed, one halfe hodgsed & two killderkinns, one flower tubb, one kneeding troff, and six brewing tubbs, one cullender, 3 sieves, two leather bottles, one lanthorne, dishes, and spoomes, with some eathen ware, one scummer, one dosen trenchers, 5li. 13s.

In the dary – Two churns, one stann, two cimnills, one tray, 4 chees moots, 3 payls, one payer of butter scales and waits, one cheese pres with smoe, milke panns, and other eathenware, 1li. 0s. 6d.

In the parlor – One beadsteadle, with curtains and valliants and rodds, one feather bead, two boulsters, two pillows, 3 blanketts, and a curverlid, chaires, one huttch, one table, and window curtains, 5li. 15s. All the pewter, 10s.

In the hall chamber – One bedsteadle, with curtains and vallyants and rods, one feather bed, two boulsters, one pillow, 3 blanketts, and a curverlid, one chaire, 3 hutches, 3 boxes, one forme, and matt and corde, 4li.

In the parlor chamber – One halfe headed bedsteadle, one flock bed, one boulster, one blankett, one curverlid, one table, one pillion and cloth, one sithe, two sickles, 1li. 12s.

In stable – Three payer of plow harnis, one payer of body harnis, 3 bitt halters, 3 hemping halters, one payer of thill bells, and one cart sadle, and three collers, one bridle, and one pannill, one shovell, one chaf sive 10s.

In the barne – One fann, one bushell, one shovell, one flaie, 4 forke, and 4 rakes, & four sacks, 9s.

In the cart house – One waggon, one dungcarte, one payer of harrows, one plow, two ladders, one mattak, two axes, two bills, one spade, one beadle & wedges, 9li.

In the yard – 4 cows and two calves, 9li.; 2 horses and a coult, 4li.; 15 sheep and 13 lambs, 3li. 15s.; 2 sows, 1li.
6 acres of wheatt, 7li.; 4 acres of barly, 8li.; 6 acres of oatts, 6li.
Wareing appearrell and mony in pocket, 1li.
The Sum Totall – 70li. 17s. (should be 70li. 14s. 6d.).
(Appraisers – Laurence Hilliard, William Clary (or Claree).)

Abraham Brecknocke of Roxwell, yeoman. 15 February 1693/4.

In the parlor – A long table, six joyned stooles, a forme, foure chaires, a livery cupbord, a small glass shelfe, an old little table, a pair of cobirons, & other little matters, 2li. 10s.

Henry May of Writtle, miller. 17 November 1693.

In the hall – One long table & 6 joynt stooles, 16s.; one little table, one forme, one press cupbard and cloth, 9s.; four chaires, 1 boxe of drawers, 6s.;

Thomas Osburne of Writtle, yeoman. 24 February 1672.

In ye palor – One long Table, 7 Joyne Stooles, 3 smale Joyne stooles, & one smale Table, 2 great joyne Chaires, 2 blew Cloth Chaires, 1 livory board & greene & greene Cloth, 2 Tent stich Cusheons upon it, 2 pairs of Cobirions, 1 Cloth presse, 2 Joyne Hutches, 1 Glass Case, 4 Cusheons, 1 standing Joine Bed with Darnix Curtains & vallents, 2 featherbeds, 2 Pillowes, one blankett, 1 Red Rugg, & 1 Trundlebedsted, 10li.

Glossary

Acanthus Often found as carved decoration on furniture, the name describes a leaf used in Classical ornament and in particular in the capitals of Corinthian columns.

Amorini Cupid figure carvings, often found on Charles II chairs.

Anthemion Honeysuckle flower ornament much favoured during Adam period.

Apron The ornamental member connecting the bracket feet on a chest of drawers, or the rail between the tops of legs on chairs and tables.

Arabesque European interpretation of Islamic design, consisting of flowing lines of interwoven foliage, scrolls and animal forms. Seaweed marquetry is an example.

Arcading A carved arch on columns or pilasters, found in England from sixteenth century and mainly as decoration to the panels of chairs and chests.

Art Nouveau A nineteenth-century style of decoration of which the main period in Britain extended from the 1880s to World War I. The languid use of curves and stylised plant shapes is distinctive.

Astragal A name given to the mouldings that form the glazing bars on furniture.

Back stool A sixteenth-century stool with a back that was to develop later into the single chair. In the sixteenth century the name 'chair' was only given to chairs with arms.

Baluster A turned support or column that is usually vase-shaped.

Bamboo Oriental cane, sometimes simulated in beech by cabinet makers of the Regency period.

Banding A border of inlay or marquetry laid in contrast with the colour and grain of the main surface.

Barley-sugar twist	A turned spiral support
Baroque	A florid development of Renaissance decoration, making use of sculptured forms and rich contrasting colour. Particularly represented in English furniture by the carved and gilded work of William Kent and other makers between 1725 and 1750.
Bird-cage	Four small turned columns that help to create the under support of some tip-up tables.
Boss	An ornament projecting from the main face.
Boulle	A term describing the special forms of marquetry particularly developed by the Frenchman André-Charles Boulle, 1642–1732. He achieved rich effects by the use of tortoiseshell, brass and other materials. Much copied during the nineteenth century.
Bracket foot	A straight foot of squared form, called an ogee foot when moulded (see 'ogee').
Breakfront	Particularly descriptive of a bookcase where the side sections are in line but the central portion of the bookcase protrudes forward.
Cabriole	A curved leg bending outwards at the knee and sweeping inwards towards the foot where it turns outwards yet again to meet the floor. The cabriole leg may terminate in feet of various forms – club, scroll, hoof, claw-and-ball, etc.
Canted corners	Bevelled corners that may be plain but are more often fluted or reeded.
Cartouche	A decorative device to form a tablet with scrolled edges, frequently used to carry an escutcheon of arms.
Caryatid	A female figure that may be used either as pure ornament or as a support.
Chinoiserie	A description of European decorative work carried out in a Chinese or pseudo-Oriental manner.
Chip-carving	Carved ornament that has been chiselled or gouged into oak furniture, usually found on very early plank constructed chests.
Classical	Greek or Roman design.
Claw and ball	A claw clutching a ball carved in wood and frequently used as a foot. Also 'ball-and-claw'.
Cluster column	Usually three turned spindles grouped together to create a decorative form of leg for chairs or tables.

Cock bead	A moulding projected from the edges of drawer fronts.
Console	A table standing against a wall supported on bracket supports or by an eagle etc. A name also given to a bracket or scroll shape.
Cornice	The moulded projection that surmounts a frieze.
Cresting-rail	The rail that joins the two uprights at the top of a chair back. Very often this rail is pierced or carved.
Crocket	An ornament in leaf or bud form that projects from a flat surface, frequently used in early architecture and in Gothic revival furniture.
Cup and cover	A term that has found favour in modern times to describe the bulbous decoration carved to resemble a lidded cup or vase. Frequently used in the description of Elizabethan furniture.
Dentil	The rectangular moulding on a cornice forming a series of teeth or blocks.
Distressed	In poor condition.
Dovetail	A joint much favoured by English cabinet makers in the joining of drawer sides, one side cut to expose wedge-shaped 'tongues', the other side cut with slots to receive them.
Dowel	An oak peg used to join timbers, and to ensure a tight fit between mortice and tenon.
Ebonised	Wood that has been stained black to imitate ebony.
Egg and dart	An ornament carved on quarter-curve mouldings in the form of alternate dart and oval shapes. (Said to be symbols of Life and Death.)
Escritoire	A cabinet fitted with drawers enclosed by an upright fall-flap used for writing.
Escutcheon	An armorial shield or the metal plate that surrounds a keyhole.
Fielded panel	A panel in which the centre is raised to project beyond the frame, or a panel in which the edges have been bevelled.
Finial	An ornament frequently of a knob or vase-shape used to surmount the uprights of mirrors, cabinets, clock-cases, etc., or at the intersection of stretchers under chairs or tables.
Fluting	A decoration of concave grooves frequently seen on columns and friezes of the second half of the eighteenth century.

Fret	Angular pattern pierced through the galleries of tables etc., or producing a 'blind decoration' when cut into or applied to the solid timber.
Frieze	The section below a cornice on a cabinet or beneath a table top.
Gadrooning	Repetitive carving in the form of an edging consisting of curved fluting or reeding.
Gesso	A preparation of chalk and size applied to furniture as a base for the further application of gold leaf.
Gilding	The decoration of a surface with gold leaf.
Girandole	Wall bracket with branched supports for candles, often with a mirror back.
Gothic	Description of an early architectural style that was also applied to furniture design at various periods.
Herring-bone	A border or inlay of narrow bands of striped veneer set diagonally to suggest the back-bone of a fish or a feather.
Husks	Representations of husks of wheat, found mainly on Neo-Classical furniture.
Inlay	Decoration to a wooden surface created by the insertion into the solid wood of a pattern of different coloured woods, or such materials as horn or ivory. Inlay is distinctive from marquetry in that it is not a veneer, but is recessed into the solid.
Japan-work	A term used to describe Oriental lacquer-work or the European imitation of it.
Greek key, Greek fret	Repetitive pattern composed of lines set at right-angles to one another, frequently used as a frieze ornament.
Laminated	Made from layers of the same or alternating materials; plywood is an example.
Linenfold	A decoration used on furniture and wall panels, consisting of vertical mouldings to resemble folded linen. Continental in origin, it found favour in England at the end of the Gothic period.
Lozenge	A diamond-shaped panel decoration, usually of the Jacobean period.
Lunette	Half-moon decoration found on later period oak furniture, or inlaid or painted during the Neo-Classical period.
Marquetry	Designs cut from veneers of various woods and fitted together to form a pictorial effect on furniture.

Mitre	The line formed at an angle of 45° by the cutting and joining of two right-angled members.
Mortice	The cavity cut into a piece of timber in order to take the corresponding projecting tenon to form a joint. Hence the term 'joiner'.
Moulding	A projecting band, often with a continuous pattern to give emphasis or relief to the edges of a cornice or table top.
Neo-Classical	Revived Classical decoration of delicate form often associated with Robert Adam and Josiah Wedgwood.
Ogee	A double curvature moulding, convex above and concave below.
Ormolu	Gilt bronze or gilded metal used for furniture mounts.
Oyster veneer	Wood used for veneer that has been cut in transverse sections from a branch of a tree and laid to form an oyster pattern.
Papier-mâché	A patent for this was taken out by Henry Clay in 1772. Papier-mâché was particularly fashionable for furniture making during the nineteenth century.
Patera	An oval or round decorative ornament, either carved, inlaid or painted, a motif of Neo-Classical origin.
Patina	The carefully polished and cared for appearance of a wooden surface that has been achieved over a long period of time.
Parcel gilt	Partly gilt.
Parquetry	A form of veneer laid in a geometrical pattern that frequently achieves a three-dimensional effect.
Pediment	The Classical triangular or carved member surmounting the cornice of a cabinet etc. Broken pediments, straight, swan-necked, and semi-circular, were all fashionable during the eighteenth century. The term 'broken' indicates that the line of a pediment is stopped before it reaches the apex.
Pie-crust	The term applied to a moulded, scalloped or carved edge around a table top, similar to the edging of fancy pastry.
Pietra dura	Italian ornamental work of inlaid marble or hard stones that originated in Florence during the sixteenth century. Mainly used for the decoration of table tops and fine cabinets.

Pilaster	A flattened column of rectangular section.
Plywood	A board made up of veneers each with the grain running at right-angles to the next, giving great strength when glued together.
Press	A cupboard in which clothes, etc., were stored.
Prie-dieu	A low-seated chair with a tall back used for prayer. The back slightly projects on either side at the top to form a rest for the elbows.
Quadrant drawer	A drawer which is a quarter of a circle in plan and is swung outwards on a pivot when opened.
Quartetto	Sheraton used this term in *The Cabinet Dictionary* (1803) to describe a nest of four small tables.
Reeding	The opposite of fluting; vertical beads raised in relief, often found on later chair and table legs.
Rococo	Style of decoration that succeeded the Baroque, using 'C' and 'S' scrolls, shells, curves and foliage in order to produce a sense of lightness and fantasy.
Roll-top	A desk closed with a flexible convex-shaped shutter. Roll shutters consisting of narrow strips of wood glued to a canvas backing are referred to as tambour slides.
Romayne work	Carved medallion heads in profile. Such decoration appears on early Tudor furniture in emulation of Renaissance originals.
Rule-joint	Found on drop-leaf tables where the joint is not square and opens and closes like the action of a pocket rule.
Sabre legs	A curved leg to resemble a cavalry sabre blade.
Scagliola	An imitation marble of plaster or gesso to which fragments of marble were added; it was capable of taking a high polish.
Scallop	Shell ornament often found on the knees of cabriole legs; the fact that this shell is an emblem of St James the Apostle, the patron saint of pilgrims, undoubtedly furthered the popularity of the motif.
Scriptor	An early description for a fall-front writing cabinet.
Seat-rails	The frame-work of the chair seat.
Serpentine	Often used to describe the fronts of furniture having an outward curve in the centre flanked by concave curves.
Spandrels	The decoration to be found in the four corners of a clock face.

Splat	The vertical support in the centre of a chair back, frequently pierced or shaped.
Split baluster	A turned baluster that has been split in halves vertically in order to provide applied matching ornament.
Spoon-back	An Americanism used to describe a 'Queen Anne' chair where the back has been shaped to fit the back of the sitter.
Stretcher	Horizontal bar which connects and strengthens the legs of tables and chairs.
Stringing	Narrow line of inlay.
Stile	A vertical member framing a panel.
Sunburst	An ornamental motif resembling the rays of the sun.
Tenon	See Mortice.
Tester	A flat canopy, usually over a bed.
Tunbridge ware	A veneer cut from woods differing in colour and arranged to form a pattern, made at Tunbridge Wells.
Turkey-work	Upholstery of knotted wools on a canvas base. Used from sixteenth century.
Turning	The use of a lathe in order to produce rounded shapes.
Vitruvian scroll	A series of scrolls reminiscent of breaking waves, used as ornamental bands. Vitruvius was a Roman writer on architecture, and his work was used as a source by Renaissance designers.
Volute	A spiral scroll of the type associated with an Ionic capital.
Wainscot	A medieval term to describe timber suitable for furniture, panelling, and wagon construction.

Index